A PARENT'S GUIDE TO
Self-Regulation

● ● ●

A Practical Framework for Breaking the Cycle of Dysregulation and Mastering Emotions for Parents and Children

Dr. Amber Thornton

ULYSSES PRESS

Published by:
ULYSSES PRESS
PO Box 3440
Berkeley, CA 94703
www.ulyssespress.com

ISBN: 978-1-64604-668-3
Library of Congress Control Number: 2024931678

Printed in the United States
10 9 8 7 6 5 4 3 2 1

Acquisitions editor: Claire Sielaff
Managing editor: Claire Chun
Editor: Renee Rutledge
Proofreader: Joyce Wu
Front cover design: Ashley Prine
Artwork: ebe_dsgn/shutterstock.com
Interior design and production: Winnie Liu

Contents

The Story of a Dysregulated Parent

"I'm so sick of this shit!" the woman yelled.

By now, her partner knew that this was code for "I need a break."

At this point, the woman knew she was yelling but could no longer control it. She marched up the stairs, the pace of her breath faster than ever. By now, her partner had already come to the rescue, consoling the child with a hug and beginning to clean up the mess that was made. Within minutes, the chaotic moment that had just led to her losing every ounce of cool was cleaned up and everyone had moved on to the next thing, except for her.

"I'm so over this! I can't keep doing this," the woman cried while looking at herself in the bathroom mirror. It was at this moment she realized that yet again, she had yelled at her child. Just the week before, she had apologized and promised that this wouldn't keep happening.

"I'm sorry for yelling. Mommy got frustrated and should not have yelled," she had said after snapping when he'd spilled his milk for the third time that day.

"It's okay, Mommy, accidents happen," her child replied, because they watched *Daniel Tiger's Neighborhood* together and have learned that accidents can happen to anyone. Apparently, these child-friendly lessons can also apply to parents.

"Next time, you can take a deep breath like this." He had proceeded to offer examples of how to take a deep breath, his tiny toddler chest moving up and down.

"I will, Baby," she had said. They had closed the disagreement with a big hug, plus more milk and graham crackers to share.

How could this keep happening, she wondered now. It was starting to feel like no matter how hard she tried, she could never stop yelling. She knew that becoming a parent was hard, but surely not everyone was constantly losing it like this. Her mind raced as she tried to retrace the moments leading up to today's big blowup.

The following week, she relayed the story to her therapist.

"I was in the kitchen, trying to get lunch together for the kids. My son asked to go to the bathroom, so I said 'okay.' I knew he was probably playing in the bathroom because he always does and was taking so long. But I didn't bother trying to investigate or check on him because it gave me more time to finish making the lunches. All of the sudden, I heard water splashing and something falling onto the floor. I was pretty sure he was safe but just knew he was doing something he shouldn't have been."

She signed deeply as she continued to tell the story, with her therapist listening intently.

"I finally walked into the bathroom and, oh my God...I just remember getting so mad!"

"What was it that made you so upset, and so quickly?" the therapist asked, seeking clarification for what exactly had transpired for her client that day.

"He was playing with the plunger!" Her face held a look of deep disgust as the image of the plunger in her child's tiny hands resurfaced.

"I immediately started yelling, 'What are you doing? Why are you messing with that?'" I had lost it! I was so upset, I didn't even take the time to listen or really hear the answer for what he was doing or why. I just knew I didn't like it, and I couldn't take it."

"It sounds like this wasn't the first straw, but rather the final one?" the therapist asked.

She looked up at her therapist with confusion on her face and said, "What do you mean?"

Her therapist replied, "Well, in your story, you said that you got upset so quickly. Often, that happens when our coping capacity has already been drained in some way."

Instantly, it felt like a light bulb had gone on and she could start naming all the situations, circumstances, conditions, or feelings that had drained her capacity to cope that same day. It dawned on her that she wasn't upset just about the plunger, but rather she was irritated by the dog barking, was stressed that they were almost out of Pull-Ups, was bothered by the volume of the television being too loud, was wondering why the television and tablets were playing simultaneously, was in pain because of a recent ankle injury, had not yet had her morning tea, felt "touched out" because her two-year-old was a little extra clingy lately, could still smell the burnt popcorn from yesterday in the trash, was concerned that she wouldn't be able to take her daily walk, and was still exhausted from the long week of no sleep because of toddler sleep regressions.

"It wasn't just about the plunger, it was literally everything in that moment," she explained to her partner that same evening.

"My therapist said I was probably dysregulated, and that's something I can work on."

It may be no surprise to you that as a clinical psychologist who's worked with parents and families for nearly fifteen years now, I often have conversations with my own clients that are similar to the one the therapist had in this story. I've been able to identify signs and symptoms of emotional or physiological dysregulation (see page 20) in parents for some time now, helping them to learn that the "blowups" always involve way more than what is on the surface. It is much more than just about the "plunger." It is often about all the other ways that our ability to cope has been degraded in any given moment. This leads to dysregulation and a host of other problems that interfere with our desire to parent from a kind, loving, gentle, and nurturing manner.

No, it probably doesn't surprise you to know that I've supported parents with becoming more regulated and present, but this may surprise you: *I am that parent.*

Despite my doctorate-level training in clinical psychology and years of expertise in supporting children and families, I have still been that parent who becomes dysregulated to the point of yelling uncontrollably at my child.

I can relate to the woman's story because her story is mine.

You may be wondering why I am willing to share so transparently about my own personal struggle as I attempt to help you. The answer is this: All of us tend to accept help and support more easily when we know that the other person genuinely understands. We are able to get vulnerable and share all the mess when we know the other person has been in the mess too.

I am standing here with you and letting you know that I genuinely understand the challenges you've had with becoming dysregulated and even turning into someone you aren't proud of. I am here with you, ready to get vulnerable and be in the mess. I have absolutely been in the deep end and I know there is a way out.

Are you ready to journey with me?

I realize that every parent is different. While my unique struggle has been yelling when I'm dysregulated, I realize that may not be your challenge. It could be that you distance yourself and shut down when you're dysregulated. Maybe you zone out into the depths of your phone, scrolling social media for hours at a time, all to keep from having to engage with what may feel like chaos around you.

Maybe you become really irritable, or what some may call "having an attitude," when you're dysregulated. It's possible that for years, you've presented with irritability to others and it's been misinterpreted as you being mean, harsh, or uninviting while the truth has just been that you're overwhelmed, anxious, overstimulated, and plain old dysregulated.

It's also quite possible that dysregulation for you looks like people-pleasing, overworking, and completely forgetting about your own needs. You forget about yourself so that you're able to care for the needs of everyone around you and so you can handle everything happening around you. Maybe dysregulation means you dig yourself deeper into the hole of "all the things" as you attempt to get it all done so you can finally feel better.

Whatever your vice may be when it comes to being dysregulated while parenting, my hope is that you see yourself in this book. I hope that by the end of reading these words, you are certain that you aren't the only parent who has struggled with being so dysregulated that you barely recognize yourself. I also hope that by the end of this book, you and so many other parents will receive everything you need to go from dysregulated to self-regulated on a much more frequent basis.

Truth is, I understand exactly what your desire is when it comes to parenting. I understand it because most parents have the same exact desire. It is to be the very best parent you can be. No, that doesn't mean perfect. Rather, it means cultivating experiences for your children that allow for optimal social, emotional, and physical development for their lives. You want to parent in ways that help you get and stay connected to your children for years to come, even after they become adults. You want to be able to look back on all the hard years that have passed and say, "I did a damn good job!"

This book will help you get there, Let me share exactly how. You're almost finished with the introduction and by now, you hopefully can see yourself in the book and feel confident that these concepts will support you. Part I of this book is all about getting you acquainted with the concepts of dysregulation and self-regulation. Here are some other things you can look forward to in part I:

- An understanding of "dysregulation" and "self-regulation"
- The various forms of dysregulation that can exist and coexist within your body
- Eight key reasons why self-regulation is so hard for parents to achieve
- An exploration of (comparing and contrasting) trending parenting approaches and ways dysregulation makes these approaches feel impossible
- A review of past parenting practices and how dysregulation was likely at the core of several of them (yikes!)
- Myths that exist in our society, keeping dysregulated parenting going (e.g., the multitasking myth)
- The four moments of time in a day when parents find themselves the most dysregulated, and what to do about it
- A conversation about what it means to re-parent yourself, realizing that your struggles with dysregulation likely existed before you became a parent and probably began in your childhoods

Part II of this book will dive deep into an independent research study I conducted with parents just like you. These parents agreed to share information about their daily life, family routines, coping skills, and most dysregulated moments. The best part is that they have also allowed me to share it all with you. Part II will:

- Outline aim, purpose, method, results, and conclusions of the research study conducted with parents about dysregulation
- Feature parent dialogue and discussions highlighting the highs and lows of dysregulated parenting, as well as opportunities for how these parents may achieve self-regulation
- Officially identify common themes, trends, and patterns in the experiences of dysregulated parents, and where to begin when it comes to taking action toward a more self-regulated approach

Part III of this book is likely what made you decide to purchase it, because it will provide the exact method for how to go from dysregulated to self-regulated as a parent. Part III will introduce the PCR (Practical, Conscious, Realistic) Method for Dysregulated Parents, the very method that helped me to finally break the cycle of dysregulation that has one time too many led to me yelling uncontrollably at my children. I'm excited about the PCR Method because it includes the most simple, accessible, and realistic strategies you can implement into your life and with your family, almost immediately. Each strategy will be reviewed in depth in part III, with examples for how you can incorporate it into your already busy or full life.

Are you ready? I'm so excited to go on this journey with you! I can't wait until you get to feel what it's like to go from dysregulated to self-regulated. I know it's possible for you, and I'm cheering you on at every step of the way.

Let's begin.

PART I

Self-Regulation and Why You Need It

CHAPTER 1

• • •

What Is Dysregulation, and Why Is the Opposite So Hard?

What comes to mind for you when you read or hear the word "dysregulation"?

Do you imagine a group of children running around yelling, screaming, confused, and crying? Because honestly, that's often what comes to mind for me. For instance, think about a classroom full of kindergartners who just came back from a field trip, except during the field trip, lunch got lost and they all missed their nap. Or think about a family with four children who just finished a ten-hour road trip to visit family, except it rained the entire drive, someone forgot to charge the tablets, and all snacks were eaten within the first two hours.

Okay, last one. Could you imagine going on a trip and leaving your children with a trusted adult for five days? You leave ample instructions for mealtimes, nap times, and morning and evening routines, except upon your return, you learn that the adult lost the list. Therefore, meals happened whenever, naps didn't happen at all, and the kids were left to fall asleep and wake up on their own time every single day.

Well, I don't know about you, but now I need to take a deep breath because the amount of chaos I just witnessed inside my mind with these scenarios is maddening, and yet, the perfect examples of what may come up when you think about dysregulation.

Dysregulation can look and feel like chaos, imbalance, disorganization, uncontrolled environments, or general dysfunction. Have you also noticed that the term "dysregulation" also evokes images or thoughts of children first? Why is that?

We will dispel several myths together in this book, and the first myth is this: dysregulation happens only to children.

The actual truth is simply, dysregulation happens to everyone—especially adults.

I understand exactly how and why this myth came to be. One way to think about dysregulation (I'll dive much deeper into the full definition later) is a loss of control or inability to control one's mental, emotional, or physiological state. We often assume that being an adult means being in full control of yourself at all times. However, I know that this expectation is far from the reality. In fact, adults experience dysregulation time and again, throughout the days, weeks, months, and even years of their lives. Become a parent and it's likely that your experiences of dysregulation could increase dramatically.

One huge reason that this book exists now is because parents become dysregulated, and yet, we don't talk about it. Not only does the myth of dysregulation only happening to children continue to persist, it's also become seen as a failure if or when an adult "loses control" of anything. As adults, we are expected to constantly have it all together. This is especially the case if you are a parent.

Parenting brings on a lot of guilt and shame regarding your beliefs, actions, and decisions. Therefore, it's not uncommon for you to feel shamed, judged, or harshly criticized for becoming dysregulated.

"How could they do that?"

"What's wrong with them?"

"What about their children?"

"If they're acting like that, how could they be a good parent?"

If you've never heard anyone say these things about you or another parent, it's likely you've mumbled them to yourself—about someone else or even about yourself.

We parents are criticized and are hypercritical of one another, including ourselves.

The myth of parents never being dysregulated continues to persist because of the shame, guilt, and fear we all experience when we become dysregulated. There is relentless internal judgment and pressure to hide what is really going on inside of ourselves.

This entire book is based on the reality that parents become dysregulated, a lot.

It is not a personal failure. There is no judgment here. This is truly a safe space to reflect on what really happens when your emotions, body, and mind are dysregulated, what impact it has on your family, why it occurs in the first place, and what you can do about it.

DEFINING DYSREGULATION, REGULATION, AND SELF-REGULATION

Now feels like the perfect time to officially define "dysregulation." First, let me say, I am an expert on this topic, but I am not the only expert. Therefore, it's possible that you may stumble across various definitions or opinions of the term that are different from my own. That is perfectly okay, and I want to make sure you and I are on the same page about what I am referring to when I'm using the word "dysregulation."

From here on out, I am defining "dysregulation" in the following manner:

Dysregulation: A term used to describe a disturbance or imbalance in normal functioning. Dysregulation occurs in situations where something or someone is not properly regulated or controlled, and this imbalance can lead to irregularities or dysfunction.

More simply put, dysregulation is a state in which people, situations, or circumstances are out of balance or not working as they should.

Dysregulation in the emotions, body, or mind can result in various problems and symptoms in regulating emotions, physiological processes, and cognitive systems. Unfortunately, many of these problems and symptoms go unnoticed or dismissed.

Now that you are aware of what dysregulation means, I also think it's important to take the time to define "regulation" too. Hence, from here on out, I am defining "regulation" in the following manner:

Regulation: A term used to describe composure, equanimity, and balance in normal functioning. Regulation occurs in situations where something or someone is properly regulated or controlled, which facilitates optimal functioning.

More simply put, regulation is a state in which people, situations, or circumstances are in balance and working as they should.

Regulation in the emotions, body, and mind can help cultivate optimal emotional equilibrium, physiological processing, and cognitive systems.

Last, because this book focuses on self-regulation, here's the definition I'm referring to when I discuss "self-regulation."

Self-Regulation: A term used to describe one's own ability to achieve composure, equanimity, and balance in normal functioning. Self-regulation occurs in situations where an individual is able to achieve proper regulation, self-control, or optimal functioning.

More simply put, self-regulation is a state in which an individual has achieved and is able to maintain balance over themselves and their own reactions or responses to the situations or circumstances around them.

One's ability to self-regulate their emotions, body, and mind is an important skill for cultivating optimal emotional regulation, physiological processing, and cognitive systems.

TYPES OF DYSREGULATION

It's possible that the term "dysregulation" may feel general and overarching, which it is. Therefore, let's also discuss the three most common types of dysregulation that will be referred to in this book.

COGNITIVE DYSREGULATION

Cognitive dysregulation can also be referred to as mental dysregulation, executive dysregulation, or dysregulation of the *mind*. This type of dysregulation involves an inability to regulate or control your cognitive and mental responses.

For example, imagine a parent has had a very hard day and is now working to put their toddler to bed. As we all know, putting a toddler to bed may be the hardest part of the day, so it is concerning to imagine a parent who is already spent now tackling the hardest part of the day; and yet, this is a harsh reality for many of us. After the events of this parent's day, they "snap" while trying to read the nightly bedtime story. The parent immediately realizes they were wrong and apologizes to the child, to which the child responds, "It's okay, it's okay to make a mistake." The child's response is evidence of the gentleness and warmth they frequently encounter at home. The parent finishes the story and says goodnight—however, while leaving the child's room, can't help but continue to ruminate over the mistake they made.

"I shouldn't have yelled like that. Why can't I just control myself?"

The parent continues to ruminate over this one moment for the remainder of the evening and into the night.

The parent's continual rumination over this incident is one indication of their cognitive dysregulation in the moment, as they are unable to acknowledge and move on from this event. They are not able to control or manage this form of response, and therefore will likely continue to feel dysregulated at bedtime and possibly in the morning.

Other signs of cognitive dysregulation include (but are not limited to):

- Focusing too much on just one thing, with an inability to shift one's attention
- Being easily distractible
- Excessive daydreaming or spacing out rather than remaining present in the moment
- Struggling to switch or transition between tasks
- Problems with impulse control
- Trouble starting, organizing, planning, or completing difficult or daunting tasks
- Challenges with listening or paying close attention
- Difficulty learning or processing new information

PHYSICAL DYSREGULATION

Physical dysregulation can also be referred to as physiological dysregulation, or dysregulation of the *body*. This type of dysregulation involves the physical body's inability to respond or regulate following stress and adversity. This type of dysregulation is also home to the infamous dysregulated nervous system.

Nervous system dysregulation has become more trendy on social media, with many therapy or mental health content creators sharing about the experiences we can have when our nervous systems are dysregulated. The nervous system is made up of two main parts: the central nervous system and the peripheral nervous system. The nervous system functions through two subdivisions: somatic, which drives the voluntary functions of the body, and autonomic, which drives the involuntary functions of the body.

Within the autonomic subdivision of the nervous system are two distinct systems:

- Our **fight-or-flight response** is regulated by the sympathetic system.
- Our body's ability to regulate our **rest-and-digest response** is regulated by the parasympathetic system.

When put all together, a regulated nervous system is a well-designed and complex system that ensures our survival by helping us to respond appropriately to stressful circumstances and threats. When your nervous system is working well, it should help you to return to homeostasis, or a balanced place, once the threat is gone. However, when your nervous system becomes dysregulated, the responses to threat or stress are no longer appropriate. A dysregulated nervous system causes you to overreact or underreact inappropriately to threats and stress. Furthermore, the body doesn't often return back to homeostasis as well or as fast. The result is that you can begin reacting to present circumstances on the basis of past stressors. At this point, your physiological perception of threat (what is happening in your body at the moment) is much different from your external reality (what is actually happening within your environment).

For example, imagine a parent who has a very busy career and lots of responsibilities at home, who also had a tough upbringing. They have been extremely proud of their accomplishments, seemingly "making it out" of the circumstances they were born into and now living a much different life. Few would even know that, as a child, they experienced lots of verbal and emotional abuse from their own parents. There were many days when they weren't sure what to expect from their own parents, as the unpredictable nature of their moods created a great amount of stress and tension. This same parent was able to graduate high school and get into college, but still seemed to find themselves in romantic relationships that mimicked some of the abusive experiences from the past. Now they are settled in a career that is fulfilling but fast-paced. They also have three teenage kids, who have moods and emotions that tend to be unpredictable and confusing (like any teenager).

Lately this parent has really been struggling with how to interact with the kids, because their children's bad moods and high emotions create a load of tension, so much so that the parent has become extremely distant at home to create space from the chaos.

Unfortunately, what this parent doesn't realize is that while the stress that comes with teenage emotions can be challenging, this parent's nervous system is dysregulated and responding as if they are still in the old abusive and harmful circumstances. Hence, even the thought of going home has led to physical and emotional distress that doesn't match up with the actual reality of what is happening at home.

Other signs of physiological and nervous system dysregulation include:
- Frequently feeling on edge or overwhelmed
- Frequently feeling snappy, irritable, or reactive
- Experiences of chronic pain and illness
- Being highly sensitive to sensory stimuli
- Frequent sleep difficulties and daytime fatigue
- Chronic attention and concentration problems
- Food cravings and appetite changes
- Emerging immune system changes or hormonal symptoms
- Skin and gut issues
- Feeling highly sensitive to other people's emotional states

EMOTIONAL DYSREGULATION

Emotional dysregulation can also be referred to as "affect dysregulation," or dysregulation of the *spirit*. This type of dysregulation involves an inability to regulate or control your emotions and emotional responses. This makes it difficult for you to soothe yourself when high or intense emotions arise, and it becomes more challenging to get back to "normal" after the feelings come up or the trigger has dissipated.

For example, imagine a parent whose child has just brought home a permission slip and information for an overnight camping trip with her school. Every year, the school hosts an overnight camping trip for the eighth-grade class to celebrate and honor their upcoming graduation. The parent knew this day would come but has avoided it incessantly because the thought of their child leaving, even for one night, has been overwhelming. The parent becomes tearful and begins to cry at the thought, even while at work and other social functions.

"I need you to sign my permission slip! Did you see it?" the child asks, but the parent continues to avoid the conversation.

"Just come sit and watch this movie with me," the parent responds.

Time continues to pass without any conversation about the trip or the permission slip being signed.

"Don't forget to sign it, I need it by tomorrow!" the child urges, as a whole month has passed, but the parent still can't find the courage to talk about this trip without breaking down.

Later that day, the parent answers a phone call while at work.

"Hello?"

"Hi, is this the parent of Shaun? I am calling about permission for the camping trip. Permission is due today and I don't want them to miss this trip."

The parent immediately breaks down on the phone.

All parents will go through periods of discomfort as their children grow and begin tackling new endeavors (e.g., overnight school camping trips), and some may discover that their emotional dysregulation could unintentionally impede their children's growth and exploration. That is the case for this parent, who had such a difficult time coping emotionally with the idea of their child going away that they avoided the situation until it was nearly too late.

Other signs of emotional and affect dysregulation include:
- Experiencing overly intense emotions
- Explosive anger
- Impulsive behaviors
- Frequent overwhelm and tearfulness
- Lack of emotional awareness
- Trouble making decisions
- Rapidly shifting mood swings
- Withdraw and isolation
- Inability to manage behaviors
- Avoidance of difficult emotions or emotional conversations
- Difficulty setting boundaries

Whew, I feel like I just finished an entire course on dysregulation. I know that was a lot of information, but by now, I hope you are starting to feel more acquainted with the concepts we will be discussing throughout this book. I also hope you are starting to identify yourself a bit in these concepts too. I want you to remember that if you see yourself in the examples, or notice that you've exhibited signs of cognitive, physical, or emotional dysregulation, you are not a bad parent. Rather, you are a parent who has endured a lot and needs new skills for how to manage and cope.

Before I end this chapter, I want to give you some reassurance and validation that much of this isn't your fault. No, it's not your fault that self-regulation has been so hard, especially after having children. However, now that you are committed to learning more about this and have a desire to make some changes, it's your responsibility to make that happen, and we can do this together. So let's quickly talk through ten reasons why regulation can be extremely challenging as a parent. This is not an exhaustive list, but rather consists of challenges that I commonly see come up for parents and may be coming up for you as well.

1. **Mental health challenges.** Did you know that the World Health Organization (WHO) estimates that approximately two-thirds of mental illnesses go undiagnosed? I can testify to the fact that there are parents who have not realized or maybe have been afraid to acknowledge that they may be suffering from a mental health condition. Mental health challenges can absolutely decrease one's capacity to self-regulate, especially when children are involved.

2. **Sleep deprivation and fatigue.** It can take up to six or seven years after having a child for a parent to regain the same sleep duration and quality that they maintained prior to having that child. The outcomes may worsen if a parent has multiple children. This makes for parents who are likely struggling with chronic fatigue and sleep deprivation, making it all the more difficult to self-regulate when needed.

3. **Overstimulation.** Parents can become overstimulated when their senses or minds become overwhelmed by excessive sensory input or mental stimulation. Too much noise, lights that are too bright, too much information, too much physical touch, or too much activity happening in the surrounding

environment can all lead to overstimulation. Sounds like a typical evening at home, right?

4. **Excessive demands and responsibilities.** With parenting comes a whole new set of expectations, from your child and also from the people and systems around you. The demands for parents are high and the responsibilities often seem endless, causing stress, worry, anxiety, and challenges with self-regulation. It becomes very hard to regulate yourself when you are constantly thinking about the next thing, which is often the case for parents.

5. **Lack of support.** A lack of support can be physical, emotional, or even financial, all of which can be detrimental for parents. Access to resources and support doesn't necessarily take away all the challenges that come with parenting, but it can help ease the load. When that support is not available, it can throw many parents into fight-or-flight mode and make it even more difficult to self-regulate.

6. **Insufficient wellness practices.** Wellness sounds good in theory; however, maintaining the practice of wellness as a parent can feel unreachable at times. Regardless of how challenging it can be to deeply care for your physical, mental, emotional, and social needs, doing so is imperative and helps to increase capacity for coping and self-regulation. Therefore, the inability for parents to access wellness practices is a growing concern.

7. **Inexperience or lack of education on coping strategies.** I don't recall ever taking a course on how to cope with the challenges and responsibilities that come with parenting. I'd also argue that even adults who are not parents struggle with

how to actually cope with life or don't have enough tools for self-regulation. Many of us simply need more education on how to access and use these strategies, and that could drastically improve our ability to self-regulate.

8. **Disconnection from self and one's own feelings.** Many adults become disconnected from themselves and their own feelings as they begin to take on more responsibilities that come with starting a career, managing finances, and generally becoming stable in our society. This disconnection can exponentially increase once you become a parent. Self-regulation requires the ability to be deeply in tune with your feelings and the signs that come along with them. Without that connection, self-regulation is almost impossible.

9. **Past traumas.** Many parents have not had easy upbringings. For those of us who may have experienced neglect, or physical, emotional, and sexual abuse in our lifetimes, there is likely healing that needs to occur or is still in process. Traumatic stress naturally impedes the process of self-regulation, which is why trauma recovery is so important. However, if trauma recovery hasn't fully occurred, challenges with self-regulation will arise.

10. **Emotional triggers in parenting.** No one prepares you for how much emotional pain or how many distressing emotional memories can resurface in parenting. Parents are expected to be able to differentiate between their own emotional triggers and the current reality, which often has very little to do with their internal emotional experience. This whole process can be extremely dysregulating, leading to decreased capacity for self-regulation.

CHAPTER 2

• • •

Exploring Parenting Practices from Yesterday and Today

Part of the conversation around parenting and how dysregulating it can be should include a review of actual parenting styles. This chapter will cover how parenting styles have changed within the last generation. More importantly, I want you to walk away from this chapter understanding how dysregulation or the capacity for self-regulation may or may not impact and influence the parenting approach.

First, we will begin exploring three common approaches from when you likely were growing up. Then, we will explore three common approaches that you likely are either hearing more about or attempting to execute with your own children. For each approach, I will be sure to highlight when the approach became popular, a brief summary of how the approach works, strategies used in the approach or common characteristics of the approach, and main criticisms of the approach. Finally, we will chat about the role that dysregulation or self-regulation plays for each approach.

Ready?

YESTERDAY'S PARENTING

AUTHORITARIAN PARENTING

Popularity: Authoritarian parenting became popular during the early 1960s.

Summary: Authoritarian parenting was identified by psychologist Diana Baumrind in the early 1960s, in an effort to understand parenting styles and their effect on child development. Dr. Baumrind characterized the authoritarian style of parenting by high levels of control and demands from the parent, with minimal to no responsiveness and warmth. Authoritarian parents are most often strict and rule-oriented, and expect unquestioning obedience from their children (e.g., they might be known to say "because I said so"). Parents who practice this approach most value discipline and adherence to authority and often use punishment as a means of controlling or managing child behavior.

Key strategies or characteristics:

- **High control from the parent.** Authoritarian parents typically have strict rules and expectations. These rules and expectations are enforced with minimal room for negotiation or flexibility.

- **Low warmth and emotional support.** Authoritarian parents generally show little affection or emotional warmth toward their children. This often leads to decreased emotional closeness and a lack of open communication.

- **One-way communication.** Authoritarian parents frequently lecture or give orders, with the expectation that the orders will be followed without discussion, compromise, or consideration for the child's feelings or opinions.

- **Punitive discipline.** Authoritarian parents resort to discipline often when their child does not meet the expectations that are set. Many times, discipline is harsh or inconsistent.
- **Focus on obedience and respect for authority.** Authoritarian parents value respect and obedience to authority figures. There is often an expectation for the child to comply without any question.

Main criticism of authoritarian parenting: While authoritarian parenting might be helpful in managing child behavior, it can also have very negative effects on child development. These potentially include low self-esteem; difficulty making decisions; lack of confidence in their own decision-making abilities; rebellion or its opposite, overcompliance; and reduced communication skills. Many of these children later go on to report experiences of anxiety, depression, lowered frustration tolerance, and a general increased occurrence of emotional distress.

How dysregulation or self-regulation is involved: Because much of the authoritarian parenting practice is rule based and emphasizes high control by the parent, it does not seem to require a high capacity for self-regulation by the parent to execute. This practice does not seem to necessitate any internal reflection or emotional processing from the parent, which makes it possible to execute consistently without the need or practice of parental self-regulation. However, I suspect that when an authoritarian parent becomes dysregulated, the severity and intensity of control or obedience required could increase. Similarly, the frequency and intensity of punitive discipline also might increase once an authoritarian parent is unable to self-regulate.

HELICOPTER PARENTING

Popularity: The term "helicopter parenting" was first introduced in the early 1990s.

Summary: The concept of helicopter parenting was first introduced by authors Foster Cline and Jim Fay. Helicopter parenting describes overprotective and highly involved parenting practices. Helicopter parents tend to closely monitor and intervene in their children's lives, often to an extreme degree. The term "helicopter parenting" suggests that these parents "hover" over their children, much like a helicopter hovers in the air.

Key strategies or characteristics:

- **Overprotection.** Helicopter parents often feel compelled to shield their children from any potential harms, discomfort, or failure, even when the child has capacity to developmentally handle or cope with said event. Helicopter parents are highly invested in protecting their children from facing challenges or setbacks.

- **Constant monitoring.** Helicopter parents closely monitor their children's activities, academic progress, social endeavors, and whereabouts.

- **Micromanagement.** Helicopter parents are highly involved in their children's daily tasks, even the ones that children are independently capable of mastering.

- **Limits on child autonomy and independence.** Because of their high level of involvement, helicopter parents limit and restrict child autonomy and independence. While some of

these limits and restrictions can be intentional, many helicopter parents may be unaware of the limiting nature of this
approach.

- **Anxiety and fear-based rationales.** Helicopter parents often
  base their actions and parenting choices on a fear of potential danger or negative outcomes for the child.

Main criticism of helicopter parenting: Helicopter parenting
has been found to have both positive and negative effects on
children and child development. While this approach may lead
to a child feeling supported or protected by their parents, it
more often than not can feel excessive and burdensome, and it
can hinder or delay child development of autonomy, resilience,
and problem-solving skills. Helicopter parenting often contributes to experiences of childhood anxiety and stress, as children
learn to have every aspect of their lives managed by parents.

How dysregulation or self-regulation is involved: It's important
to note that not all parent involvement is negative. It's extremely
important for parents to have a visible and consistent presence
and level of involvement in their children's lives. However, the
component of fear and anxiety characterized by helicopter
parenting is what concerns me most and leads me to believe that
helicopter parents may also be dysregulated parents too. For
many parents, dysregulation can manifest as fear and anxiety.
While fear and anxiety are common emotional experiences felt
by parents, it becomes a concern when these same fears and
anxieties begin to drive parenting decisions, which are a major
component of the helicopter parenting approach.

CORPORAL PUNISHMENT

Popularity: The use of corporal punishment has been practiced for centuries across various cultures, but data indicates that its use and level of social acceptance began to significantly decline toward the end of the twentieth century.

Summary: Corporal punishment is not necessarily a distinct parenting approach, but rather has long been seen as a staple practice for many parents over the past centuries. Corporal punishment involves physically disciplining a child through actions like spanking, hitting, pinching, or slapping. Corporal punishment can also involve the use of indirect physical force, such as forcing a child to hold fixed postures for long periods of time. Parents who use corporal punishment often believe that physical punishment is the best way to instill obedience and respect for authority in children. These parents frequently use corporal punishment to help enforce discipline, teach children right from wrong, or manage undesirable behaviors. It is important to note that shifts in the social acceptance of corporal punishment and increased research regarding the effects of corporal punishment have led to the implementation of several laws and policies that restrict or ban its use. However, the use of corporal punishment may still persist in some cultures or societies.

Key strategies or characteristics:

- **Physical contact.** Corporal punishment requires physical contact with a child in order to administer punishment.

- **Punitive intent.** The primary intention of corporal punishment is to inflict pain or discomfort as a consequence for a child's perceived misbehavior. This practice is meant to discourage a child from repeating the behavior in the future.

- **Immediate response.** The use of corporal punishment tends to be administered immediately after an undesirable behavior occurs, with the goal of creating a direct association between the behavior and the punishment.

- **Authority based.** The practice of corporal punishment heavily emphasizes the authority of a parent or caregiver. The practice assumes that a parent or caregiver has the right to physically discipline a child in order to maintain obedience and control.

- **Coercion and fear.** The use of corporal punishment also invokes fear and intimidation. Many parents who use corporal punishment believe that the use of fear and intimidation can also improve compliance and obedience.

Main criticism of corporal punishment: The use of corporal punishment has been widely debated, and more recently, child development experts and advocates have strongly recommended against its use. New research on the long-term effects of corporal punishment indicate that there are grave negative outcomes for children, such as increased aggression, lowered self-esteem, higher levels of anxiety and depression, and impaired parent-child relationships. Additionally, research has also shown the use of corporal punishment to be an ineffective solution for long-term behavioral modification in children.

How dysregulation or self-regulation is involved: The practice of corporal punishment is similar to authoritarian parenting in that it does not seem to require a high capacity for self-regulation from parents. Rather, the concern becomes how much the use of corporal punishment may intensify if or when a parent is dysregulated. For instance, it seems possible that if a parent who uses corporal punishment is dysregulated, this could result in physical punishment that is intensive, more severe, and even abusive. It seems very possible that a parent who is unable to regulate their experiences of anger, frustration, anxiety, sadness, or even fear could begin to use these dysregulated emotional states as fuel for their use of corporal punishment. Dysregulated emotional states becoming the driver for corporal punishment could and has been devastating for many children.

TODAY'S PARENTING

POSITIVE PARENTING

Popularity: Positive parenting started to become popular in the late twentieth century.

Summary: Positive parenting (also known as "positive discipline" or "positive reinforcement parenting") is a parenting approach that focuses on nurturing a strong and respectful parent-child relationship. This approach heavily promotes the child's development, self-esteem, and general well-being. Positive parenting helps parents to focus on and emphasize communication, understanding, and teaching vs. punishment. The goal of this approach is to create a positive environment that nurtures the child's whole self, and it is believed to have positive long-term outcomes, which include adequate coping and adjustment in adulthood.

Key strategies or characteristics:

- **Mutual respect.** Positive parenting encourages the parent to see the child as an individual with their own thoughts, feelings, and opinions that warrant respect and consideration.

- **Clear expectations and boundaries.** Positive parenting involves setting clear and age-appropriate expectations and boundaries for behavior. This helps children to know what is expected and what is acceptable.

- **Positive reinforcement.** The practice of positive parenting deemphasizes punishment and instead focuses on rewarding and reinforcing positive behaviors, (e.g., via praise, encouragement, and rewards).

- **Effective communication.** Open and honest communication between parents and children is highly encouraged in the positive parenting approach. This helps parents to actively listen, validate feelings, and provide nonjudgmental guidance.

- **Problem-solving and conflict resolution.** Positive parenting aims to teach children problem-solving skills and help them understand the consequences of their actions. Conflicts are frequently resolved through discussions and collaborative solutions.

- **Consistency.** Positive parents understand the importance of consistency when applying rules and consequences. This helps children learn that there are consistent outcomes for their actions and about the concept of "cause and effect."

- **Empathy and understanding.** Positive parents strive to understand their children's perspectives, feelings, and needs.

This helps create and nurture their emotional connection and sense of security.

- **Modeling desired behavior.** Positive parents lead by example to help demonstrate the behaviors or attitudes they want their children to learn.

- **Nonviolent discipline.** The practice of positive parenting strongly rejects the use of any physical punishment or harsh discipline in parenting.

- **Focus on long-term development.** Positive parents are highly motivated to learn and prioritize the long-term development of their children. This includes their social, emotional, cognitive, and behavioral growth.

Main criticism of positive parenting: Despite research citing the positive long-term benefits of positive parenting, critics remark that the approach is too time consuming and demanding when compared to other parenting styles. Positive parenting also does not yield immediate results like authoritarian parenting or corporal punishment might. Rather, it is the consistency and long-term use of the approach that yield results. Critics of the approach also worry that too much focus on nurturance and fewer punishments could lead to permissiveness or over-indulgence vs. accountability and consequences. Last, positive parenting does not provide immediate control over a child's behavior, which is often deemed socially unacceptable in many societies.

How dysregulation or self-regulation is involved: Unlike most of yesterday's parenting practices, positive parenting requires a high capacity for self-regulation. This parenting approach is complex because the parent would need to have a full understanding of concepts such as positive reinforcement. It would also benefit parents to have some knowledge of child development to properly know what to expect from their child's behavior at any given age. This approach requires consistency, dedication, and commitment, even when your child's misbehaviors may be testing you. Therefore, one can imagine how challenging positive parenting might be after a long day of work, on a bad day, or when you're sleep deprived. Parents who struggle with feeling dysregulated likely would find this practice particularly difficult.

GENTLE-PARENTING

Popularity: Gentle parenting started to gain prominence in the late-twentieth century.

Summary: The gentle-parenting (also known as "attachment parenting" or "respectful parenting") approach emphasizes building strong, nurturing, and respectful relationships with children while promoting their emotional well-being, autonomy, and healthy development. Developing strong emotional bonds are at the core of this parenting approach, and because of that, gentle parents are keenly aware of the value of empathy, understanding, and noncoercive discipline methods. Gentle-parenting also acknowledges that parenting can be hard as well as complex, yet the need to foster a positive parent-child relationship based on respect, trust, and emotional connection is still great.

Key strategies or characteristics:
- **Unconditional love and acceptance.** Gentle parenting is rooted in a high regard for unconditional love and accep-

tance for children. It emphasizes that a child's worth is not contingent on their behavior.

- **Empathy and understanding.** Gentle parents strive to understand and empathize with their child's feelings, needs, and perspectives, while also prioritizing open communication and active listening.

- **Positive discipline.** Gentle-parenting focuses on teaching and guiding child behavior through positive discipline techniques, such as redirection, natural consequences, and problem-solving discussions.

- **No punishment or harsh discipline.** Gentle-parenting rejects punitive and coercive methods of discipline. Rather, gentle parents aim to address behavior with understanding and respectful communication.

- **Respect for autonomy.** Within the gentle-parenting practice, children are regarded as individuals with their own thoughts, emotions, and autonomy. Children are involved in decision making and their choices are respected whenever appropriate.

- **Secure attachment.** Gentle-parenting emphasizes building secure attachment bonds between parents and children. This helps to provide a foundation of trust and emotional security.

- **Child-led learning.** Gentle parents support their children's natural curiosity and interests, allowing them to explore and learn at their own pace.

- **Modeling desired behavior.** Gentle parents aim to model the behaviors and values they want their children to adopt.

- **Emphasis on emotional intelligence.** Heavy emphasis is placed on helping children develop emotional intelligence within the gentle-parenting approach. This involves recognizing and managing emotions effectively.

- **Parenting self-care.** The importance of self-care for parents is highly valued by gentle parents. These parents are encouraged to prioritize their own well-being to better support their children.

Main criticism of gentle-parenting: While gentle-parenting is generally embraced by parents and recommended by experts, critics argue that the parenting approach is too permissive due to its overemphasis on understanding and empathy. Critics often believe that too much understanding and empathy might interfere with a child's preparedness for "the real world," which may be more harsh or challenging. Similarly, there is a concern that gentle parents might not provide enough clarity and consistency when it comes to boundary setting. Critics also note that gentle-parenting is time-consuming, doesn't immediately produce behavioral change, and can be demanding for parents and interfere with their own well-being.

How dysregulation or self-regulation is involved: Similar to positive parenting, gentle-parenting also seems to require a significant capacity for self-regulation by parents. Gentle-parenting relies heavily on a parent's ability to be present, provide empathy, and model ideal behaviors. However, all of this is extremely hard to do when we are dysregulated and can't seem to get a handle on managing our own fatigue, frustration, anxiety, etc. Therefore, gentle parents who also are able to identify when they are feeling dysregulated and able to use skills or strategies to self-regulate likely feel more confident and secure when using this approach.

CONSCIOUS-PARENTING

Popularity: The conscious-parenting approach started to gain popularity in the late-twentieth century.

Summary: Conscious-parenting (also known as "mindful parenting"), is a parenting approach that emphasizes being fully present, aware, and intentional in your interactions and decisions as a parent. It is rooted in principles from mindfulness practices and psychology and encourages self-awareness to create a deeper and more meaningful parent-child connection. This approach calls for parents to slow down and tune in to their own emotions in order to make intentional choices that prioritize emotional well-being, empathy, and positive communication. Conscious parents firmly believe that their ability to provide mindful awareness and emotional intelligence can lead to even more positive parent-child interactions and better emotional and behavioral outcomes for children.

Key strategies or characteristics:

- **Present-moment awareness.** The conscious-parenting approach encourages parents to be fully present and engaged with their children in each moment, rather than being distracted by external concerns or preoccupations.

- **Self-reflection.** Conscious parents are encouraged to apply self-reflection and self-awareness to understand their own triggers, emotions, and reactions. Doing so helps parents to respond to their children in a calm and thoughtful manner.

- **Emotional regulation.** Conscious-parenting emphasizes managing one's own emotions and reactions, which allows parents to respond to their children with empathy and understanding rather than impulsiveness or emotion.

- **Empathic communication.** Conscious parents create safe spaces for their children by practicing active listening, empathy, and nonjudgmental communication.

- **Positive discipline.** The conscious-parenting approach advocates for nonpunitive discipline methods that focus on teaching, guiding, and setting clear expectations for behavior. Rather than punishment, problem-solving and cooperation is promoted.

- **Modeling behavior.** Conscious parents are encouraged to model the behavior they want to see in their children. They do this by modeling emotional intelligence, respect, and understanding .

- **Embracing imperfection.** Conscious parents understand that parenting can be a challenging journey with ups and downs. Therefore, parents are encouraged to approach parenting challenges with self-compassion and a willingness to learn and grow.

- **Cultivating gratitude.** The conscious-parenting approach practices gratitude and appreciation for the joys and challenges of parenting.

- **Mindful decision-making.** Conscious parents make deliberate and thoughtful decisions about their parenting choices, always considering the long-term impact on their children's well-being.

Main criticism of conscious-parenting: Many of today's parenting practices seem to have similar criticisms, such as lack of consistent boundaries and unclear expectations, an overemphasis on children's needs, being too time-intensive, limited preparation for "real world demands," and risks of permissiveness. These same criticisms are also associated with conscious-parenting.

How dysregulation or self-regulation is involved: Of all of today's parenting approaches reviewed, conscious-parenting seems to be most dependent upon a parent's ability to identify and manage their own dysregulated states. Without this ability, conscious-parenting is more likely to feel frustrating, too challenging, and close to impossible.

THE BIG CONCLUSION

Someone out there is reading this who has felt really depleted, frustrated, ashamed, and disappointed in themselves because they find the parenting approaches of today (positive parenting, gentle-parenting, and conscious-parenting) to be extremely difficult. This parent has internalized this belief that "something must be wrong with me" because "no one else seems to be struggling with this like I am" when in fact, so many of us (including me) are struggling with staying the course with these new parenting approaches.

The parenting approaches of today offer promises of healthy, optimal, and positive long-term development for our children, and I know we all want that. However, many of these approaches do not often explain how much a parent's well-being and ability to recognize their own regulatory states play a factor in how well they are able to execute the practice. Instead, parents who struggle with the strategies that come with positive, gentle, and conscious-parenting are left feeling as if they don't have what it takes to be a good parent today because these approaches aren't coming easy.

Parenting is hard enough but to also feel as if you are failing your children because you're struggling to grasp a parenting approach that you know can be great for them—sucks. You don't need that much pressure to add to the already long list of things you need to ensure get done each day. Instead, I want to offer this: trust that this book will help you to get closer to where you want to be with these practices because it will help you get to the core of the problem, which is dysregulation.

No, you aren't failing because you can't seem to stop yelling or don't seem to have the capacity for empathy as much as you want. No, you aren't failing because you zone out every evening to protect your sanity. No, you aren't failing because you're too anxious to give your kids the autonomy they really need. No, you aren't failing because *now insert whatever it is you're struggling with when it comes to any given parenting approach.*

You're not failing; you're just dysregulated, and we can fix that.

CHAPTER 3

• • •

Societal Ideas That Encourage Dysregulated Parenting

Have you ever thought about the world we live in and how it may keep us in a dysregulated state? Or, if it doesn't keep us in a dysregulated state, it often encourages us to become less regulated. A certain type of hustle and bustle comes with adulthood, which then seems to triple when you become a parent. We all have largely normalized the conditions we live in when it comes to busyness, productivity, expectations, and the demands placed upon us. It's heavy, right?

I've often talked to parents who've internalized this idea that they are failing, not a good parent, or simply not good enough, all because they can't measure up to the extremely high demands and responsibilities placed upon them, not only from their children because, well...they are children, but also from the world and people around them. Everyone has an opinion about what should be done for a child or as a parent. Even if they aren't speaking to us about those opinions, we know they're there. They're in the air at the park, in the friendly small talk and brief conversations in the school pick-up lines, in the questions people ask at dinner, and also in the practices we tend to pick up or hold as a society.

The society we live in has a major impact on how we then parent, for better or for worse, and unfortunately, none of us are immune from it. It takes a lot of intention, consideration, and courage to go against the grain of a society when it comes to questioning practices, beliefs, or trends, especially around parenting. Honestly, we may not even have the mental capacity to question any of this because we are simply trying to get from day to day the best we can. However, deep down inside we feel that something may be off or just not aligning well with how we may actually want to live or be.

That brings me to two ideas that have become staples in our society and that only lead us to becoming more and more dysregulated. Both ideas create a vicious cycle of you trying to fulfill the expectations of the idea, failing because it's unreasonable, becoming dysregulated, this then negatively impacting you and your family, then you trying to fulfill the expectation of the idea again because you believe you need to try harder. The cycle continues until you are exhausted, jaded, and unfulfilled, and your kids are now in therapy because your dysregulation has gotten so out of control...okay, I'm kidding with that last one. I know that may be one of your biggest fears (it's actually mine too) so let's not go there just yet.

The point is, you need to identify these ideas so that you gradually become more aware of when they are at play in your life, then work toward some changes. This chapter can be the start of that process for you.

1. THE MULTITASKING MYTH

I grew up with the idea that multitasking helps you to be more productive. When I was in college, it seemed that the most successful students were the ones who were multitasking with everything. It wasn't enough to do just one thing, and multitasking made it possible for them to do a lot more. Of course you can watch TV and finish your essay! Why wouldn't you listen to music while reading your chemistry textbook? Everyone is eating and studying together. Yes, you can be the president of five organizations at the same time.

Multitasking was also a heavily utilized skill for my peers in graduate school. With increased academic demands and more responsibilities, multitasking became much more than a skill and rather a need to get through every daunting semester. You could even see it in the professors who were, for the most part, our first mentors and leaders in the field. They were constantly juggling multiple courses, proposals, grants, research projects, manuscripts, etc.

Then came parenthood. The need to multitask rose exponentially. I believe we really saw this come to play during the COVID-19 pandemic. In 2020, many families were forced to hunker down in their homes and do everything together, for months. Many parents quickly needed to find ways to continue to work and be productive on their jobs from home, while also helping their child attend virtual school and keeping up with the general day-to-day of home life. The pressure was intense and multitasking seemed like the only option.

There's also this prevailing idea that women are "natural multi-taskers" and should be able to handle a multitude of tasks or events simultaneously. So when a woman becomes a mother, she is looked upon to manage an almost never-ending list of responsibilities and demands that are impossible to do without multitasking in some way. Furthermore, she is expected to do this without any impact to her mental health, physical health, or family relationships—all without failing.

The truth is that multitasking carries several negative consequences, most of which impact the ability to self-regulate. Studies have proven over and over again that most instances of multitasking actually seem to reduce productivity, which is contrary to what most of us were taught about multitasking. Multitasking requires constant switching between tasks, which can be taxing for the brain, as it needs more time to refocus and adjust with each task change. With that, it's also been found that multitasking lowers the quality of work, impairs the ability to concentrate, increases mental fatigue, and increases stress.

More importantly (at least for the purposes of this book), multitasking creates a cognitive strain that can interfere with your ability to manage and regulate other parts of yourself. As you continue to read this book, you will learn that self-regulation does, in fact, require a great deal of capacity, effort, intention, and focus. However, when this same capacity, effort, intention, and focus is used to multitask, all bets are off that you'll be able to regulate yourself after your child has just spilled all of their spaghetti on your new shoes.

2. THE PERFECTLY RESPONSIVE PARENT MYTH

Prior to becoming a parent, I recall reflecting a bit on what my childhood was like. I thought about all of the times that I felt my parents "missed the mark" on or lacked understanding for how I was feeling. I considered the times when I believed my parents could or should have done something different. I then decided that I would do a much better job to fully understand and adequately respond to the physical and emotional needs of my children.

You too?

Now when I think back on this as a parent, I have to laugh a bit because on one hand, yes, my approach to parenting does lend toward me being able to have a better approach for how to understand and respond to my children. But on the other hand, I still get a lot of this wrong. I still miss the mark. I've had several moments when I've felt like I've already made so many mistakes in my children's short lives so far, or that I've already "messed them up."

Those fears run deep, and I'm still messing up. The mistakes haven't stopped. Every single day, I say or do something that isn't ideal, and then, much later, after the event has passed, I realize there was a better way that I could have handled the situation. I've assumed that these mistakes would not happen if I was intentional, reflective, and extremely considerate as a parent, but now I'm learning that isn't necessarily true.

Just like I believed my effort or intentions to be the best parent I could be would protect me from making most or any mistakes, there is a larger societal idea that you need to be a perfectly responsive parent in order to raise children who are well developed and optimally adjusted. To add to this idea, it is assumed that if you give your all to parenting and contribute great effort and intention to be the best parent you can be, you will make few mistakes. However, the actual reality is that you still may make a lot of mistakes, regardless.

Imagine you're a new parent with a newborn, and you've bought this idea about the perfectly responsive parent. Your ideas about how you wanted to parent prior to your baby being born involved being available, present, emotionally connected, and providing every single need or desire your child may have. This was your goal and intention from day one; however, now you are headed toward day forty-five and feeling exhausted, drained, mentally checked out, emotionally raw, and generally unsupported. Your baby has been crying nonstop for the last thirty minutes, and despite your biggest desire to attend to every single cry, you know that if you don't step outside to gather yourself at this moment, you may lose it for good.

You decide to stick it out and stay present and attentive, not realizing that you are completely burned out and have isolated yourself from your partner, friends, and family who have offered to help. You haven't showered in days and you've begun to lose weight because you aren't eating. Still, your biggest goal is to be the best parent you can be.

Similarly, imagine that you're a parent with a teenager, and you also bought this idea about the perfectly responsive parent. Your ideas about how you wanted to parent prior to having children involved being available, present, emotionally connected, and providing every single need or desire your child may have.

This was your goal and intention from day one; however, now that you are approximately sixteen years in, you are feeling defeated, worried, frustrated, and rejected. Your teenager hasn't openly talked to you about their life in months, and despite your biggest desire to soothe and respond to every concern or issue they may encounter, you haven't been able to get your teenager to open up this time. You know that if you continue to push, you might risk pushing them too far.

You decide to try one more time to get them to talk, but your teenager lashes out and demands that you leave them alone, but forever this time. You break down, feeling even more rejected and fearful of what may happen if you can't help them, yet you haven't realized that your teenager has been asking you for space for months now and your inability to grant them the safe space to process their own feelings has negatively impacted your relationship with them a great deal. Still, your biggest goal is to be the best parent you can be.

Striving to responsively meet your children's needs perfectly is unreasonable and leads to several negative consequences, all of which have dysregulation at the root. When you are unable to manage and regulate your own physical, cognitive, and emotional states, you will eventually begin to notice massive declines in your physical health and mental health, as well as disruptions in relationships with your children and family. While there is never a guarantee that you won't face challenges as you raise your children, your ability to manage and regulate yourself during the process leads to more years of healthy and positive development for you and your family.

BREAKING THE CYCLE OF DYSREGULATING PARENTING MYTHS

I wonder what it might be like if the practices and ideals that our society upholds truly helped to keep us stable, comfortable, and satiated as parents. How might things be different? This is not to say that there aren't structures, practices, resources, or even policies already in place to support parents; however, more work could be done.

This extra work that is needed needs to go deeper. This next step requires a deep restructuring of how we think about our lives as adults and then as parents. Some of this work may require actively and directly rejecting some of the old lessons and ideals you were given, and then to create your own. I imagine this next step of the work may also feel messy, because rejecting all you've known and creating something new can feel scary, vulnerable, and even lonely. This book is an invitation to begin that work, because your capacity to self-regulate so that you can continue to be a safe, loving, and nurturing presence for family truly depends on it.

CHAPTER 4

• • •

Daily Dysregulation

By now, you know what dysregulation means. You've learned about all its forms. We have explored parenting styles and their relationship to dysregulation. We have even explored some myths in society that keep our dysregulated states going. We have covered a lot of ground so far, and yet, there's still so much more to cover. But first, how often do you believe dysregulation occurs for most parents? Should we make this a quiz? Yes, I think so.

Okay, here we go.

Pop quiz: How often does dysregulation occur for most parents?

A) Once per season, B) Once per month, C) Once per week, D) Once per day, or E) Multiple times per day.

Drum roll please.

If you guessed A, I'd love to know who your children are and what your secrets might be because I feel like you need to be writing this book instead. If you guessed B, I'd also love to know how you manage to regulate yourself better than the literal rest of us. If you guessed C, you're well on your way to becoming a self-regulated superstar and that still feels pretty magical. If you guessed D, I can tell you're being pretty reasonable and yet still underestimating the amount of dysregulation that occurs for parents.

However, if you guessed E, then you are my people and you absolutely have guessed correctly. Round of applause to you.

Okay, now that the fun is over, let's get real. There are multiple opportunities within the course of a day for a parent to experience dysregulation. Yes, multiple opportunities, meaning more than one. In this chapter, I will cover three major times of day, plus one period of the week, that tend to reduce a parent's capacity and ability for self-regulation. In addition, I will also talk about one specific time of year when you will likely notice experiences of parental dysregulation really spike.

Let's start from the top.

THE MORNING HUSTLE

Good morning.

Your alarm has just gone off and you know that you have a full day ahead. Your list of tasks and responsibilities is long, and you need to get started now to be ahead by the end of the day. You take your first step out of bed and realize that gone are the days when your mornings involved only you. If you're anything like me (and I know you are, because you're reading this book), you have children and they are a major part of your morning.

Depending on the age or developmental stages of your children, the stress or dysregulating quality of morning time can range, and for many parents, this part of the day is when the chaos begins. This is particularly the case from Monday through

Friday, also known as "the work week." The challenges of a morning with kids absolutely ring true for working parents, but mornings can also be a struggle for stay-at-home parents, especially those who work from home or generally need to handle other responsibilities throughout the day.

It's reasonable to expect that most humans need a period of time in the mornings to wake up, get out of bed, move their body, or simply rehydrate from the night of sleep. However, when you became a parent, what used to be a gentle start to the day became aggressively harsher and could very well have felt like a huge electric jolt. It's possible that you're no longer afforded the time you once had to yourself in the mornings, as many children wake early and have needs that begin instantly. It's also likely that you're having to stretch an already limited amount of time to make sure that everyone is ready and out of the door at a very specific time. Double the dysregulation points if your child is not yet ready for independence and requires 100% of your assistance. Special mention for the parents whose children are independent but still rely on your executive functioning (which is likely already compromised) to get from A to Z at 6 a.m.

See how the dysregulation begins?

Time pressure and high demand are two significant qualities of a morning that seem to contribute to dysregulation for most parents. Having a limited amount of time to get a lot of things done can easily lead to hurry, urgency, imperativeness, and panic. Unfortunately, these states are also associated with emergency and crisis, which can lead the mind and body to believe that you are in a state of emergency or crisis from the start of each day.

THE "SECOND SHIFT"

Ah, the evening is here.

It's likely that you've just completed a long day at work. Or maybe you kept the kids in line for most of the day at home. Now it's time to transition to the evening. You probably remember a time when you felt a sense of relief as the clock slowly moved closer to 4 or 5 p.m. You knew that all that was waiting for you once you got home was a leftover chicken meal with maybe a half pint of ice cream. Oh, and your favorite show to binge until you fell asleep on the couch. Or maybe your evenings used to consist of hitting the gym, or meeting friends for a happy hour and staying out until you felt tired. You had time and flexibility to wind down as needed after a long day, and enough space to recuperate before the next. However, now it's quite possible that instead, a new wave of dread creeps in because your "second shift" will soon begin.

Whether you know it as the second shift, "5 to 7 shift," "4 to 7 shift," "the witching hour," or even "family time" (shout out to the parents who are able to look at this with a glass half full), parents know this time period all too well as the time that requires a level of energy that you genuinely do not have to give. Instead of moving into a calmer, lighter, or more flexible phase of your day, the second part of your day might become more chaotic, time consuming, and possibly even more demanding than the typical work day.

The second shift implies that you are checking in to yet another period of work, and for many parents, leaving work and coming home between roughly the hours of 4 to 6 p.m. can feel exactly that way. The biggest challenge of this shift is fatigue, and as a result, limited coping capacity. It seems reasonable to expect that a typical work day (this includes our stay-at-home parents, because caring for children is also work) will drain or deplete the average adult of physical, mental, and emotional resources, which is why the happy hours, pints of ice cream, TV binges, evening naps, or general enjoyment of choice after a work day are so appealing. These activities help to rejuvenate and restore any energy or fuel lost from the day. However, parents are not afforded those same luxuries, and finding creative ways to restore lost energy from the work day is extremely challenging.

It's no wonder that many of us find ourselves snapping at dinnertime or right before bed. We are literally drained of anything we've had left and desperately waiting for the day to end.

THE MIDNIGHT HOUR

You're awake, except it's not morning just yet. You roll over to look at your phone and realize it's 2:12 a.m. Yikes. You recall a time when you were able to roll back over, feeling reassured that you still had at least three or four more hours of sleep left. It was easy to fall right back to sleep and wake up rested and ready for the day ahead. If not, you may have gotten up to get a snack from the kitchen or simply watched some TV until you were able to fall back asleep. Sleep was much simpler back before parenthood.

Now it's 2:14 a.m. and you're awake because you feel a light tugging on your side of the bed and hear a small voice saying, "I'm scared of the monsters." You immediately get up, take a deep breath to conceal your frustration, and walk the little one back to bed, maybe even reassuring them that everything will be okay. Meanwhile, you are panicking inside with the idea that you only have three or four more hours before your alarm goes off, and you know it will take you at least one hour to fall back to sleep.

That particular scenario may not be identical to yours. For you, a newborn might be getting up every two to three hours for feeding and comfort. It could also be that your young toddler is going through a sleep regression and is waking up again after months of sleeping well through the night. Or perhaps your school-age child is having some anxiety about a social situation, and it's keeping them up at night. It might even be that your teenager is convinced that they need to stay up until after midnight because they "aren't tired yet." Whatever the case, it's a challenge when it's after midnight and your children need you but you'd much rather be sleeping.

Dysregulation is common when you're sleep deprived, and an astounding number of parents have disrupted sleep for months or even years at a time. It can be common for parents to experience challenges with physical regulation in the midnight hours. This could manifest as increased blood pressure, dizziness, fatigue, temperature fluctuations, or even restlessness or jitteriness. Emotional regulation can also be compromised, as many succumb to anxiety about being awake, irritation with their children for the waking, or even frustration about their inability to fall back to sleep or experience regular, restful sleep.

THE WILD WEEKEND

It's the weekend!

You made it through a long week and now it's finally time to let loose. You may not be the "partying" type, and that's okay, because all you want to do is rest, relax, and quiet your mind after it's been on the go for days. Or maybe you want to go enjoy someone's party, game night, or social activity, or meet up with a few friends. You know it's been a while, and after the week you've had, this is something you not only need but also deserve. However, right as you are envisioning the weekend you'd like to experience, you get an alert on your phone about the birthday party invite your kids received weeks ago. Not only that, you also remember that it's your weekend to grocery shop for the family, and there's a huge load of laundry that you've been putting off.

So much for that time to relax and unwind.

Parents understand the struggle that is the weekend. A two-day pause each week to rest, relax, and enjoy some freedom or flexibility from responsibilities suddenly became a two-day race to ensure children get their social needs met, groceries are shopped for, laundry is done, family time has happened, and all else is prepped for another busy week ahead. The honest truth is that for many parents, the weekend can feel more busy, hectic, and challenging than a typical work week.

While family time with children can be sweet and full of enjoyment, it also can bring high emotion, overwhelm, overstimulation, as well as physical and mental fatigue. All of this can lead to quite a few dysregulated parents just trying to make it to Monday. The weekend often requires a great deal of executive functioning in order to implement structured activities or planned events into the two days, which can help many parents navigate the time. However, if you're already exhausted from a long work week, the last thing you may want to do now is plan what will happen for the family during the weekend.

The other alternative is to truly sit back, attempt to relax, and let go. This approach can be relieving for some parents who don't have the mental energy to plan for the weekend, or for those parents who physically don't have the stamina to keep up with the weekend. However, other parents struggle with the anxiety and restlessness that can come with this approach, often feeling as if they should be "doing something" or more easily getting overstimulated by children who are also attempting to occupy their own time during an unstructured time period.

I suppose another approach is to secretly daydream about the days when the children are all grown and away so that you can do whatever it is you want to do on the weekends. But I know you don't ever think about that. How could you ever dream about a time when the children are finally out of the house? We know that isn't allowed.

Absolutely kidding. Dream away, especially if it gets you through any wild weekend.

BONUS: SUMMER BREAK + BACK-TO-SCHOOL

I went back and forth about whether to include this section about summer breaks and the back-to-school season. However, as I was in the process of planning and writing this very chapter, my family was knee-deep into summer, with back-to-school right on our heels, and I could tell we were all feeling the pressure. I'll explain.

It feels counterintuitive to say that summer break is one of the most dysregulating time periods for parents, because isn't it supposed to be fun? Summer break implies that there is a break or pause from all the things that we may have been obligated to get done or responsible for doing. It's supposed to be the ultimate moment of freedom, enjoyment, and satisfaction. This is exactly how I remember summer break as a kid. An entire three months (have you noticed how short summer breaks are now? I digress) of fun, excitement, and good times. Then came parenthood.

I truly didn't realize what the experience of summertime felt like for parents until I found myself desperately searching for summer camps for my toddler because he had just completed his first year of "big boy school," and childcare for him was no longer a thing after the conclusion of an academic year. It was intense.

Don't get me wrong, my family and I got to have a lot of fun this summer. We traveled twice to spend time with family who live far away. We visited new museums. We stayed up late at friends' houses and played in pools. We had ice cream for dinner some nights. We had good times, but I noticed that the unpredictable nature of summer, in addition to the flux in schedules, routines, and my children's energy levels, made for some challenging moments. I also noticed this in other parents. Peak summer for parents is venting to your other good parent friend about how you can't wait until school resumes, all the while knowing that deep down, you will look back on the summer memories and still smile.

It's almost like a beautiful chaos that is sure to return the following year.

Then, of course, there's back-to-school, which sometimes feels like the dark cloud trying to intrude on the summer fun. The reminders for back-to-school season go out early, and for many parents (including myself), they trigger this endless list of tasks that need to be completed prior to the first day of school. Anticipating our children's return to school can also bring on big emotions for everyone, such as sadness about the summer ending, anxiety about what to expect with a new school year, uncertainty about how the academic year will progress, resistance to resuming old routines for dinner and bedtime, etc.

Going from the flexibility and fluidity that can come with summer to the routine, structured, and planned nature of back-to-school can feel jarring. Parents are doing their best to make sure the children are prepared and simultaneously trying to re-implement months-old routines that haven't been in place since the last school year ended. All the while, the first day of school isn't the end of the destabilizing period, as it sometimes takes weeks or months for a child or family to adjust to a new school year.

This is a reminder to give your fellow parent acquaintances some grace if they seem a bit stressed and out of sorts in tomorrow's school drop-off line. They are likely navigating a lot right now, just like you.

CHAPTER 5

• • •

Re-parenting Ourselves for Better Regulation

If there's one thing you and I have in common, it's this: we are trying our literal best to give our children the most positive, healthy, safe, enjoyable, and well-rounded experience imaginable in this life.

No, that doesn't mean they will have all the things. It doesn't imply material luxury or even perfection. You won't necessarily take a ton of trips or vacations. Rather, intentionality in parenting can make a huge difference, even when you make mistakes or get things wrong.

Something that parents today have become extremely well-versed on is how important it is for our children to be provided space and emotional safety to experience their "big feelings." We all know that children come with big feelings and sometimes their expression of those feelings are a little intense. There's lots of yelling, crying, screaming and of course, tantrums. Sometimes there is anger and frustration directed at you, when you were the last person to be involved in whatever has gone wrong. These big feelings also may not subside quickly and can last for what feels like hours.

Many of us didn't get the warning of how challenging making space for our childrens' big feelings can be. It requires time, patience, mental capacity, emotional capacity, and compassion. However, as the first four chapters of this book helped to explain, most of us are susceptible to moments of dysregulation due to a variety of factors. That means that regardless how intentional you are in making space for something so important, it will be a challenge. Possibly one of the biggest challenges and most triggering tasks of your parenting experience.

However, here comes the internet yet again to the rescue. The internet is full of tools, strategies, and parenting influencers and experts (some of you may have even found me there too) all trying to guide and support parents in what it means to make space for our children's big emotions. It's likely that you've gravitated to a few of those people or resources, looking up to them when it comes to support for how to navigate this particular task. You try on and lean into many of the tips they provide, and you even find some of them to be helpful, but you can't help but to feel something that is hard to explain. Eventually you find yourself wondering what it would have been like to have these tools, strategies, and techniques be a part of your upbringing as a child so that you could have had your big feelings too.

What does it mean for an entire generation of parents to be providing support and emotional safety for big emotions when they, themselves, were never given the space?

This is complex because many of us may feel a sense of pride and excitement knowing that we are shifting the norm when it comes to how we parent and raise our children. We are well aware of the developmental and relational benefit of gently supporting our children's emotional growth, no matter how challenging it is. It's a huge accomplishment to break a cycle of hindered emotional safety and then turn it around to create emotional safety in abundance. It might even feel like your greatest work as a parent. On the other hand, it can be extremely hard to give your child something that you never were able to receive, all while finally realizing that you desperately needed it too.

You and I deserve a lot of grace for this very reason: we are passionate and committed about providing a level of care to our children that we probably did not receive.

Now let me clarify—this does not necessarily mean that our upbringing was bad or wrong. It's quite possible that our parents also did their very best in caring for us and providing us with a positive, healthy, and cheerful experience. It's also very possible that our parents were generational curse- and cycle-breakers in their own right. This makes me think a lot about my parents, who both grew up in the rural South with very little, only to ensure that we had a lot more. That was huge for them, and their efforts do not go unnoticed at all. Similarly, I'm sure you probably have your own story about what your parents were able to provide and the ways you are grateful for them.

Simultaneously, it's okay for you to feel some loss, sadness, anger, frustration, confusion, resentment, or any other emotion as you learn about the parenting practices you never had the privilege to experience. It is okay to feel all of that, especially if you are noticing how the lack of this emotional safety is still affecting you as an adult.

One huge reason why self-regulation is so hard for many of us and why dysregulation is so common is because those skills were not taught when we were younger. Not only were they not taught, I believe many of the parenting practices from before really hindered our ability to adequately identify, understand, and cope with regular, everyday feelings. No, this isn't because our parents didn't love us. It's not because they didn't try. It reminds me a saying by Maya Angelou: "When you know better, you do better," and our parents didn't know what we know today about the value and long-term effects of healthy emotional expression and safety.

As you learned in chapter 2, parenting practices have evolved tremendously over the years. You've likely noticed that with each generational progression, mental, emotional, and psychological well-being have become a much bigger priority. That's amazing for our children but does leave many of us in a sticky situation, as we now are understanding that the reason why parenting can be so challenging at times is because regulating our physical, mental, and emotional selves is something we were never intentionally taught. The good news is, I don't believe it's too late, and this is exactly what this book is for.

Let's close this section of the book out with a chat about re-parenting.

REWORKING YOUR RELATIONSHIP WITH YOURSELF

You have probably gone around in circles trying to parent in ways that are unfamiliar to you. You've hit some bumps in the road and have probably been very hard on yourself. There may have been days or nights when you wished you had the same gentle guidance or deep compassion that you are also trying to give to your kids. It may feel like that's no longer an option for you, but it is, and I want to show you how effective re-parenting can be, especially on this journey to self-regulate.

You deserve every ounce of joy, compassion, gentleness, and ease you are working to provide to your children. In fact, you absolutely need it in order to plant the seeds of self-regulation for yourself. Because of that, I want you to begin to think of this process as your own re-parenting journey. One that will lead you to less dysregulation and much better self-regulation.

Re-parenting is essentially a process that allows you to heal and rework the relationship that you have with yourself. Most commonly, this is in the context of addressing childhood issues or wounds, such as not being allowed to fully express your emotions as a child, not being allowed to speak up about what you need, not being able to receive adequate empathy and compassion, etc. Re-parenting can feel empowering because you are no longer left to rely on individuals who genuinely aren't able to provide what you need. Instead, you get to figure out how to break free from any negative influences of your past childhood experiences and build a new healthier one, with the current adult version of yourself.

Here are some important re-parenting principles to keep in mind as you continue this journey:

1. **Healing childhood wounds is important.** Re-parenting focuses on identifying and addressing emotional, psychologi-

cal, or developmental wounds that may have occurred during one's upbringing. These wounds can stem from experiences such as neglect, abuse, or emotional unavailability from caregivers. Similarly, many adults struggle with self-regulation because of these same wounding experiences. Throughout this process, embrace what healing these wounds may look and feel like for you.

2. **Self-compassion is required.** Re-parenting encourages individuals to develop self-compassion and self-care by learning to nurture themselves as they would a child. I often find myself wondering how parents are supposed to provide nurture and compassion if they haven't first received it themselves? If we take this a step further, it may not be enough to simply have received nurturance and compassion as a child. Nurturance and compassion needs to be continuous throughout adulthood and one's parenting journey, like a flow of water. This involves treating yourself with kindness, empathy, and understanding, especially when you've made a mistake.

3. **Re-create your own healthy parental role.** In re-parenting, you are encouraged to become your own nurturing and supportive "inner parent." This means providing yourself with the love, guidance, and validation you may not have received as a child. I know that so far, you may have only done this with your own children, but now is the time to make sure you are being a good parent to yourself as well.

4. **Identify and challenge negative patterns.** Part of the process of re-parenting, involves recognizing and changing negative patterns of thought, behavior, and self-talk that

may have developed as a result of past experiences. You will notice that these negative patterns of thought often feed or influence how you react and respond to your children's big feelings. You will also begin to notice just how much these negative patterns of thought are directed toward you, especially in the moments when you believe you aren't living up to what is expected, when you get things wrong, or when you are not feeling confident as a parent. I hope that this book will help you to challenge self-criticism, perfectionism, and self-sabotage as you gain more empathy, understanding, and self-compassion.

You've come this far. Let's keep going.

PART II

It's Not Just You: Unearthed Secrets of Dysregulated Parenthood

CHAPTER 6

Self-Regulation in Parenting: A Research Study

Have you ever wondered about the struggles of other parents? Specifically, have you ever wondered about whether it's a challenge for them to stay patient? Do they fight to keep their cool and not lose it? Are they zoning out in the evenings during dinner too? Do they feel like self-regulation is close to impossible most of the time?

I have wondered the same things too. With every struggle I have as a parent, I often ask, *Is it just me? Am I the problem? Or can I feel reassured that millions of other parents are also struggling just like me?*

Essentially, we all want to know that we are normal. We want to be reassured that our issues are just part of the everyday struggle and not something that is flawed or wrong with us. We want to feel validated in the mess so that it feels just a little bit better.

I believe every parent needs that, because the drive to self-blame, feel guilt, or torment ourselves over our mistakes is great and doesn't allow for us to truly show up effectively for the children we love so much. While our deepest desires may be to love, cherish, and provide a healthy environment for our children, we are often swept away mentally and emotionally by every single moment that we get it wrong. It takes us out of the moment and into a space that isn't conducive for healing or growth. No parent deserves that.

Throughout part II, I will share with you everything I learned from 175 parents about what it feels like for them to become dysregulated, the challenges they face with self-regulation, the tools and strategies they've tried, and what their biggest worries and concerns are about their inability to regulate. My hope is that you will see yourself in these parents while learning a bit from their experiences too. My hope is that this portion of the book will get you thinking even more and reflecting much deeper about the source of your struggles with dysregulation, because it's very difficult to change things when you don't understand their origin.

I also hope that this portion of the book allows you to further drop your guard and embrace the imperfections that make you who you are. May this portion serve as a reminder that you don't have to be the perfect parent, but rather a parent that continues to try your best, all the while knowing that your best will never mean perfect.

SELF-REGULATION IN PARENTING: A RESEARCH STUDY

In July of 2023, I set out to learn as much as I could about parents and their experiences with being dysregulated while they parent. I shared with my social media audience that I was studying dysregulation and its impact on parenting well-being, and I invited any parent to participate in my Self-Regulation in Parenting Research Study.

The Self-Regulation in Parenting Research Study offered me an opportunity to be the curious psychologist that I am while also being the loving parent who also struggles with when and how best to regulate myself. I've been able to look through, read, and speak to parents about a number of their challenges, biggest fears, difficult feelings, and immense concerns about what all this means. As I work to put all the words and sections of this book together for parents just like you, I realize that I'm not sure if I could have done so without these two major parts of me: psychologist and parent.

Like you, I've had my concerns about what my inability to self-regulate at times would mean for me and my family. Because I've had my own concerns about this, I decided to make sure to ask the parents in the Self-Regulation Parenting Research Study about their own concerns. I had a feeling that aside from the talk about what dysregulation looks like, how it feels, when it happens most, etc., parents also just generally had concerns about the impacts of their dysregulation.

Prior to participating, every participant fully understood the study's purpose to gain insights into dysregulated parenting, its causes, and its effects on both parents and children. I let study participants know that their survey responses and interview responses would contribute to the understanding of dysregulated parenting behaviors and the development of strategies for supporting parents in need.

The bulk of information I received was through an online survey made up of eighteen questions that asked about the parents, their background, their children, their environment, their parenting approach and emotional well-being, and of course, their experiences with dysregulation.

I was fortunate to get 175 responses to this survey within 30 days of it circulating online.

Following the initial survey, I asked the same survey participants to join a focus group where I would ask more in-depth questions within a smaller, intimate group setting.

I ended up conducting two focus groups that included a total of sixteen parents.

This focus group was probably the highlight of the entire study, because the conversations with parents about this very topic were unlike any I've heard before. The rawness and realness of the comments and responses shared helped me realize even more why we need to be talking about dysregulation and what it means for parents to seek strategies for better self-regulation and emotional mastery. It's imperative for our mental health and the quality of our relationships with our children. Furthermore, the healing nature of validation and knowing you're not alone in your struggles should never go unnoticed.

THE PARENTS

The first set of questions within the survey was all about the parents who would be responding and participating in my survey so that I could understand how their lives, environment, characteristics, and other factors impacted their experiences of dysregulation, self-regulation, or mastering emotions.

Here's what I learned:

Parenting status:
Parents were asked to identify their "parenting status," choosing from the following options:

- "I am a mother."
- "I am a father."
- "I am a parent (gender nonbinary, gender expansive, gender-queer, etc.)"

I believe it's safe to imply that those who identify as mothers likely also identify as women, while those who identify as fathers likely identify as men. Furthermore, it felt important to me to include a category for nonbinary parents.

Of the 175 parents who participated in this research,

- 93.1% (163) were mothers.
- 5.7% (10) were fathers.
- 1.1% (2) identified as nonbinary parents.

Number of children:
Parents were asked how many children they currently have. The breakdown looked like this:

- 45.1% (79) had one child.
- 33.1% (58) had two children.
- 18.3% (32) had three children.
- 2.3% (4) had four children.
- 1.1% (2) had five children.

Developmental stage of children:

The following breakdown summarizes the ages of the children of the surveyed parents:

- 9.7% (17) had infants (0 to 12 months old).
- 46.9% (82) had toddlers (1 to 3 years old).
- 45.7% (80) had preschoolers (3 to 5 years old).
- 28.6% (50) had children in early childhood (6 to 8 years old).
- 16% (28) had children in middle childhood (9 to 12 years old).
- 12.6% (22) had adolescents (13 to 18 years old).
- 3.4% (6) had adult children (18+ years old).

Relationship status:

Of the many options to choose from, parents identified their relationship status in the following ways:

- 72% (126) were married.
- 12% (21) were single.
- 4.6% (8) were divorced.
- 3.4% (6) were cohabitating/living together with a partner.
- 2.9% (5) were separated.
- 2.9% (5) were in a relationship.
- 1.7% (3) were engaged to be married.
- 0.6% (1) described their relationship status as "other."

Age:

The ages of the parents who were participating in this study were as follows:

- 34.3% (60) were between the ages of 23 and 34 years old.
- 60.6% (106) were between the ages 35 and 44 years old.

- 4.6% (8) were between the ages of 45 and 54 years old.
- 0.6% (1) was over the age of 55 years old.

Level of education:

Parents reported the following on their level of education:

- 46.9% (82) have received a master's degree.
- 28% (49) have received a bachelor's degree.
- 9.1% (16) have received a doctorate degree.
- 7.4% (13) have completed some college.
- 5.7% (10) have received a professional degree (MD, JD, etc.).
- 2.9% (5) have received an associate's degree.

Work status:

The work status of surveyed parents was as follows:

- 73.1% (128) were employed full-time.
- 8.6% (15) were self-employed.
- 6.3% (11) were stay-at-home parents.
- 2.3% (4) were employed part-time.
- 2.3% (4) were unemployed but actively seeking employment.
- 2.3% (4) were freelance/contract workers.
- 1.7% (3) were students employed part-time.
- 1.7% (3) identified their work status as "other."
- 0.6% (1) was a student, not employed.
- 0.6% (1) was retired.
- 0.6% (1) was disabled or unable to work.

Family income:

The family income level for each parent broke down as follows:

- 21.7% (38) reported a family income of $200,000 or more.
- 17.1% (30) reported a family income of $150,000 to $199,999.
- 22.9% (4) reported a family income of $100,000 to $149,999.
- 6.9% (12) reported a family income of $90,000 to $99,999.
- 4% (7) reported a family income of $80,000 to $89,999.
- 7.4% (13) reported a family income of $70,000 to $79,999.
- 5.1% (9) reported a family income of $60,000 to $69,999.
- 4.6% (8) reported a family income of $50,000 to $59,999.
- 4.6% (8) preferred not to report their family income.
- 1.7% (3) reported a family income of $40,000 to $49,999.
- 2.3% (4) reported a family income of $30,000 to $39,999.
- 0.6% (1) reported a family income of $20,000 to $29,999.
- 1.1% (2) reported a family income of less than $20,000.

Race/ethnicity:
Last, each parent identified with race or ethnicity in the following ways:

- 72.6% (127) identified as Black/African American.
- 21.1% (37) identified as white/Caucasian.
- 3.4% (6) identified as Hispanic/Latinx.
- 1.1% (2) identified as Asian/Asian American.
- 1.1% (2) identified as multiracial/mixed race.
- 0.6% (1) preferred not to indicate their race or ethnicity.

THE BIG SELF-REGULATION QUESTIONS

Next came the big questions about what it is like to self-regulate as a parent. To begin to understand parents' ideas about self-regulation, how they define dysregulation, and what it all looks and feels like to them, the survey proceeded with three fairly simple questions.

1. As a parent, how difficult have you found it to self-regulate?

The majority of the parents (approximately 69%) found it to be moderately difficult to self-regulate now as a parent. Another 20% have found it severely difficult to self-regulate as a parent, with the remaining 11% having mild difficulties with self-regulation.

2. In parenting, how would you rate your ability and/or capacity to self-regulate?

With this question, I specifically wanted to know how compromised their ability or capacity might become in any given parenting moment. The majority of parents (approximately 64%) rated their ability and/or capacity to self-regulate as a parent moderately compromised. 19% rated their ability and/or capacity for self-regulation as severely compromised, and the remaining 17% rated their ability and/or capacity for self-regulation as mildly compromised.

3. How much has becoming a parent impacted your ability and/or capacity for self-regulation?

The results of this question were telling in terms of what happens when we become parents. With this question, I was curious to know if becoming a parent has made the ability and/or capacity to self-regulate better or worse, or if has it stayed the same.

The results were clear and spoke to a resounding impact that parenting has had on one's ability and/or capacity for self-regulation. Only 6.8% of the parents indicated that their ability and/or capacity for self-regulation was mildly impacted by becoming a parent. A much larger 34.3% reported a moderate impact because of parenting, and a whopping 58.9% of parents reported a severe impact on their ability and/or capacity for self-regulation after becoming a parent.

If you've ever questioned or doubted yourself because you couldn't seem to handle things like you used to before becoming a parent, I hope you are beginning to catch on to the larger pattern here. Parenting has been hard on many of us.

LIKE PARENT, LIKE CHILD?

During the completion of this survey, I began to think a lot about what these parents were probably like as children. What were their dreams and interests? What made them laugh? What made them scared or worried? More importantly, what were their relationships like with their own parents, and were their parents dysregulated too?

I closed out the survey with one final question in order to determine if the parents surveyed witnessed any forms of healthy self-regulation in a parent as a child. I had them choose which best describes their own personal experiences going up:

• "I grew up seeing good examples of optimal self-regulation from the adults around me."

• "I did NOT grow up seeing good examples of optimal self-regulation from the adults around me."

To my surprise, I learned that only 21.7% (38) of the parents said that they grew up seeing good examples of optimal self-regulation from an adult around them. The remaining 78.3% (137) of parents were not as fortunate, as they did not grow up seeing good examples of optimal self-regulation from the adults around them.

This result specifically made me consider the importance of social learning and subsequently unlearning. Social learning theories imply that learning is a dynamic process influenced by our social interactions, observations of others, and several environmental factors. It only makes sense to conclude that much of what we witness from our parents' behaviors, we then go on to learn and mimic in our own lives. But what does it mean if we've acquired less-than-ideal ways of living, being, and coping from our parents and the environment around us? Could it be possible that our challenges with dysregulation have been learned over time and in part, need to be unlearned?

I believe the answer to be yes.

Finding yourself in a state (or multiple states) of dysregulation doesn't have to be a terminal condition, and your decision to go on this journey with me has already begun to unlock this unlearning process that you are not realizing needs to happen.

I'm so excited for you to learn even more through the experiences of these parents.

Let's keep going.

CHAPTER 7

Today's Honest Look at Dysregulated Parents

If you could get a small glimpse into the living rooms of everyone else at 6:27 p.m., what do you think would be happening? Would a parent in that family be screaming too? Or is that parent desperately counting down the moments until their kids' bedtime? Are they hiding in the bathroom with a glass of wine?

Because remember, we all just want to be reassured that "It's not just me." So I believe we all would take that peek into someone else's life if we could, simply to feel okay about the things we dislike or to keep from feeling uncomfortable about ourselves.

I know you have spent a lot of time lately thinking about dysregulation when it comes to yourself, but I want to give you an opportunity to step away from so much self-focus and actually be able to take that peek into another parent's living room.

Are you ready?

THE FOCUS GROUP FOR DYSREGULATED PARENTS

For the 16 parents in the Self-Regulation in Parenting Research Study focus group, I asked a total of four questions about their experiences of dysregulation and attempts at self-regulation, with the ultimate goal to fully listen and learn, and to share all of that learning with you.

This and the next few chapters will begin to highlight and integrate the findings and results from the larger survey, as well as the smaller focus group. It will feel like you have a nice cozy seat right in the middle of their living room. You will get to take a step out of your own head and into the life of another parent who is also struggling with many of the things you are struggling with.

"WHAT DOES DYSREGULATION LOOK OR FEEL LIKE TO YOU?"

It's not enough to talk about the word "dysregulation" in general. Instead, we need to better understand what this term looks and feels like for others. Here are the biggest themes that emerged:

IRRITABILITY, FRUSTRATION, AND ANGER

For many of the surveyed parents, dysregulation looked and felt like irritability, frustration, and anger. One of the biggest behaviors they often referenced was yelling. For them, yelling was an unintended result of feeling so irritable, frustrated, or angry in the first place.

Here's more on that in their words:
"For me, it's always in my tone. I can hear it in my tone and I know I have to fix it. But my tone changes. It's so easy to start raising my voice because I'm angry."

"I often find myself just yelling, trying to get compliance."

"Dysregulation looks like me being really irritable, frustrated, and really feeling very uneasy. It's very uncomfortable and I'm all over the place. I'm generally not a nice person during this time."

"For me, it's rage. Irritability, rage, anger comes out. I just feel out of control. Even if it's internalized, it's this feeling like I can't take it. It's a pressure that just blows."

IMPATIENCE

A lack of patience was another common experience during dysregulated moments. This category is somewhat similar to the previous category of irritability, frustration, and anger, but the lack of patience had a particular impact on the ability to communicate and guide children effectively. For example, could you imagine what it might feel like to be a parent who is already feeling dysregulated but your five-year-old wants to practice tying their shoes two minutes before you all need to head out for the morning?

Here's what some parents had to say about impatience:
"The biggest thing for me is that lack of patience. I try really hard to be calm and patient when I'm directing or redirecting but when I'm overwhelmed and dysregulated, I'm a lot more short and then I don't like that I'm being short and I get mad at myself. I'm just really impatient."

"I can notice the difference. When I am patient, I get down to their level, I speak softly, I explain things; but when I'm feeling impatient, I start expecting them to know what they need to do and don't explain or remind them calmly. There's more of like, 'We brush your teeth every day! This is not an option. Just do it!' The patience is gone. It's just not there and it affects how I'm able to communicate, explain, talk through the steps or find creative ways to help them. All the access to those tools falls away."

OVERWHELM AND OVERSTIMULATION

The experience of overwhelm and overstimulation was also common. Often, the two would go hand in hand, with "overwhelm" often feeling like more of a cognitive experience (i.e., "I have too much to do and it's causing me to feel overwhelmed") vs. "overstimulation," which tended to be a more physiological experience (i.e., "There's too much going on around me and it's causing me to feel overstimulated").

Here's how some of the parents described these experiences: "Sometimes I just want to separate myself from everyone at home, if I can."

"When I'm dysregulated, I become sensitive to all of the sounds. All of the sounds are affecting me and it's not allowing me to focus or concentrate."

"It starts with being overwhelmed and then goes into me being irritable. I'm overwhelmed and just want some peace to myself. Then I find that I'm just overstimulated by everything around me, and you can't get away."

"My anxiety is through the roof. It makes me feel like I can't do anything. I have this long to-do list and I can't do any of it because I'm so overwhelmed."

HYPERAROUSAL AND OTHER PHYSICAL REACTIONS

Last, the experience of hyperarousal was common when describing the most dysregulated moments. Hyperarousal can be thought of as a state of heightened physiological and psychological arousal. Most commonly, we see this occur in individuals who are responding to a perceived threat or stressor. When someone is in a state of hyperarousal, their body and mind become more alert, reactive, and prepared for a "fight-or-flight" response. This means that for many parents, the experience of simply being with their children can elicit a stress response that may feel difficult to control:

"I'm constantly pacing. I can't sit still."

"When I'm overwhelmed or dysregulated, I do not want to be touched. My kids want to rub my arm or touch my leg and I just do not want [them] to do that. It becomes harder to regulate when there's the constant touching."

"Mine starts with an anxious feeling. My children rely on me a lot for their regulation, so for me it is very physical first. I find myself getting anxious, I feel my heart racing. I don't yell or get angry but it's more the physical feeling in my body."

"Anxiety and feeling scared, panicky. I get fearful."

"I feel exacerbated, like nothing is going right. Even if half the things are going well, it feels like nothing's going right, and then I start to spiral into judging myself harshly. I tell myself 'I can't do anything correctly' and then the anxiety kicks into me feeling like I'm a terrible parent."

"IN WHAT MOMENTS DO YOU FIND IT MOST DIFFICULT TO SELF-REGULATE?"

Beyond what dysregulation looks and feels like, the next question aims to get a better sense of when dysregulation actually happens. Parents were asked to reflect about the moments when they find it most difficult to self-regulate or seem to have the biggest challenges, and how frequently these moments seem to occur.

Several patterns and themes emerged, leading me to narrow the responses down to three distinct moments when dysregulation is most likely to occur.

1. PARENTING AND FAMILY CHALLENGES

Many parents found it most difficult to self-regulate when there was some sort of family or parenting challenge occurring. Based on what we've learned so far, this makes sense because family and parenting challenges can bring about uncertainty, unclear resolutions, and a host of emotional reactions, many of which might be distressing. Furthermore, these challenges can be daunting, stressful, and pull from resources that we simply do not have.

Child behavioral concerns:
- "When my child will not listen after multiple requests. I don't feel heard and my voice is disregarded.
- "When my five-year-old continuously pushes boundaries and refuses to follow directions."
- "When I feel unsure what to do during a tantrum."

- "When my kid ignores directions for the fifth plus time, even with rewording and redirection. Or matters of immediate safety."
- "When my child is screaming and struggling to regulate, I feel triggered with anxiety and sometimes it takes time to regulate my emotions to then assist and guide her."
- "When my children are self-regulating poorly."

Parental overwhelm:

- "When I am feeling overwhelmed between work, school, and all the other tasks, my child keeps calling me for attention."
- "When my children are whining/crying and wanting to be held/cuddled nonstop and I am irritable due to lack of sleep and a constant state of feeling overwhelmed."
- "When I am overwhelmed or stressed with everyday life activities—school, work, housework."

Morning and evening routines:

- "End-of-day meltdowns, seemingly without reason, and meal-times, especially picky eating."
- "Evening time going into bedtime routine."
- "Attending my family's needs during morning routines, dinner/bedtime routines."
- "Generally, the entire end-of-day routine. My capacity to deal with screaming, whining, chaos, mess, noise, and resistance is significantly diminished on a good day and completely wiped out on a bad day."

Morning and evening routines:

- "In the mornings getting kids ready and getting off to work, evenings when I have to cook, do homework with them, give baths, etc., all while they are all asking questions."

Disrupted family routines:

- "Summer break!"

- "When I am working and have my child at the same time, and when my child's routine is disrupted (mostly involving when she has extra screen time)."

- "Weekend visits with their dad interferes with sleep time, morning time, all of it."

- "When my spouse is deployed and I'm solo parenting."

- "When things don't go as planned. When I am running late and when I feel like I am the only one putting in efforts in daily house and child tasks."

Demanding child needs:

- "When all children want my attention at the same time or back to back."

- "During irrational reactions of negotiating, tantrums and even everyone is asking/expecting something from me at once (spouse and kids)."

- "Attending to my children's needs during morning routines, dinner/bedtime routines, or anytime, I find it hard to be a mommy, cook, a partner to my husband, and take time for myself."

- "When I am feeling overwhelmed between work, school, and all the other tasks, but she keeps calling me for attention."

Demanding child needs:

- "When I am trying to complete a task for myself but the kids don't understand that and demand my attention for themselves. This can be asking for a ride somewhere, money, or just simply asking me to purchase them something."

- "When I need to be doing something else productive AND my child needs my attention at the same time. It feels like constant pulling in multiple directions and renders me absolutely unable to focus on either."

Communication challenges:

- "When my son has challenges communicating his needs."

- "When they are crying, whining, struggling to communicate a need."

- "When she whines a lot instead of using her words."

Partner/co-parent disagreements:

- "Whenever my husband and I are not on one accord. It makes it harder to deal with parenting problems and pretty much anything else."

- "When I am upset or stressed about something that is happening with my partner or around the house."

- "It's challenging when I'm having to compromise with my child's father and it doesn't go well."

- "I often feel like I am the only one putting in efforts in daily house and child tasks."

- "During times I have to deal with co-parenting drama."

2. LACK OF PARENTAL WELL-BEING

Another consistent and notable theme that emerged regarding moments of dysregulation involved a lack of parental well-being. It was clear that when these parents weren't feeling or doing well, dysregulation was a much more likely occurrence. Likewise, the capacity for self-regulation became severely limited when parents were not healthy and well. All parents know the struggle of maintaining your well-being while also maintaining the needs of a family, but a lack of parental well-being could also impact the family as a whole.

Here are a few areas where well-being was most impacted.

Limited "me time" or personal space:
- "At night when he takes his time going to bed and I'm tired or it's 'cutting into' my personal time. I'm in need of alone time, but I do not have the opportunity to have it."
- "When my older child is encroaching on my personal space in a way where he is purposely trying to annoy me (e.g., rolling on me, laying all over me, etc., after I have asked him not to)."
- "When the kids are whining, and I'm tired because I haven't had time to myself."
- "Every time I want to go somewhere alone the kids want to come and I find it hard to say no."
- "When I'm feeling touched out."

Fatigue and sleep deprivation:
- "When my sleep is interrupted—either early morning, late nights, or when trying to nap."
- "I find it most difficult to self-regulate when I am tired."
- "When I'm exhausted."

- "When I am tired, things feel extremely difficult."
- "When I am feeling burnt out from lack of sleep and high demands from the day."
- "When I'm super sleep deprived and my kid is having a tantrum."

Physiological/physical health concerns:
- "When I'm tired, hungry, or not feeling well."
- "When I'm tired after a challenging long day or when I'm feeling very ill."
- "When I am hungry."
- "When I'm physically not feeling 100%."
- "Hormonal fluctuations make it difficult to self-regulate."

Mental and emotional health concerns:
- "It's hard to regulate myself when I'm already upset."
- "When I'm already stressed about something or feeling flooded and my child yells at me or is also flooded and impatient with me. I'm working to not take it out on them and then they're dysregulated as well."
- "When I am tired or frustrated with something that has nothing to do with my children."
- "I struggle the most when I'm feeling stressed."

Mental and emotional health concerns:
- "Times of anxiousness."
- "I find it most difficult to self-regulate when I am already having negative emotions unrelated to parenting. Adding parenting on top of those times makes it difficult to keep my composure."

3. DISRUPTED ROUTINES AND ENVIRONMENTAL CONCERNS

The final big theme that emerged involves the disruption of daily routines and times when there are concerns with the immediate environment.

Here are the most frequent examples related to routines and environments.

Overly stimulating surroundings:

- "During times where one or more of my children is crying/yelling; when I don't want to be touched but my children want to lay on me."

- "It is difficult to self-regulate when I am hearing lots of screaming or whining at that moment, especially after being alone with the kids all day."

- "Everyone communicating with me at the same time. It feels like overstimulation coupled with exhaustion."

- "Loud and/or heightened noises."

Overly stimulating surroundings:

- "When my child is crying, when my child is whining, and the environment is overwhelming."

- "End of the day, if the TV is on and the dog is barking, and it's just generally very loud."

Running late or time pressure:

- "When I'm feeling under pressure, like something has to get done so we can leave the house."

- "When we are running late or I feel pressured to do something/be somewhere."

- "When I am running late and then feel like I'm the only one putting in effort to get the kids ready on time."
- "When we are on a schedule or feeling pressed for time."
- "Time-sensitive activities or while getting ready to leave the house."

Work-related routines and demands:
- "When I am working and have my child at the same time."
- "When things are especially stressful at work."
- "I have experienced several challenges at work over the past few months, which has severely impacted my ability to regulate when parenting becomes difficult."
- "When I have big things professionally that I know require significant time and attention, but I can't focus because my kid is being a kid."

• • •

Well, you finally got to take that glimpse into the living rooms of other parents, and I hope that now you realize, it's not just you.

Yes, dysregulation may look different for every parent, but it also happens to every parent at some point in their journey. Likewise, every parent will have a certain moment or circumstance that seems to trigger dysregulation more than others, and that's okay. The more you are able to move beyond the fear or concern that it's only happening to you, the better able you'll be to begin seeking out the right tools and solutions that work for you. You're that much closer to becoming the present, patient, and self-aware parent that you want to be.

• • •

CHAPTER 8

Difficult Emotions That Don't Seem to Pass

Whenever I accidentally yell or snap at my kids, I have a process for uncovering what has just passed. After I've been able to regulate myself and my emotions, I take a step back and ask myself: *What really happened?*

I'm usually able to backtrack and get to a point that has very little to do with my children. Usually, I find that I am already tired or feeling fatigued. Maybe I was anxious or worried about something. Maybe I was focused on something else so my attention was divided. Maybe I was already feeling uncertain about my parenting, or it's possible that I was still upset about something my kids had done earlier.

What I've come to notice is that dysregulation often runs deep and has very little to do with what's happening on the surface, as I think the parents we've been learning about have been showing us.

There are so many other factors that contribute to your ability or capacity for self-regulation. While much of this can be managed in various ways (which we will finally get to in part III of this book), you have little control over the rest (yep, I will talk about that part too). However, there's this other piece that we still need to discuss about the cycle of dysregulation, and it's called feelings.

"HOW HAS YOUR INABILITY TO SELF-REGULATE MADE YOU FEEL?"

I was overwhelmed by the immense depth of feeling that parents were able to articulate in response to this question.

In addition to feeling dysregulated because of fatigue, work challenges, high family demands, and sleep deprivation, parents also carry the weight of some pretty negative emotions because of these challenges. Many have grown to perceive themselves in a less than ideal manner and unfavorable light because they can't seem to regulate themselves enough.

Feeling like you aren't good enough or not doing well as a parent carries a heavy weight. I know you have had your own moments of self-doubt as a parent. Just remember that this experience is universal.

Next I share ten emotional states and an internalized belief that dysregulated parents tend to associate with each. I know you will be able to identify yourself in at least one of them (if not all).

1. FRUSTRATION

Frustration feels like an inner tension or agitation that comes about when you're feeling stuck or hindered in your efforts to parent well. At times, this frustration can lead to a desire to change or improve your situation (e.g., like buying this book for help). Other times, frustration can manifest as a chronic irritability that has the potential to negatively affect your relationships with others, especially your children.

An internalized belief that is often associated with frustration for dysregulated parents is "I am not effective." This belief that we are not effective as a parent, despite our best efforts, can elicit a frustrated emotional state that can linger for a long time. This sense of frustration was captured well in a statement from one of the parents interviewed:

"I get a frustrated feeling, especially in times when I'm struggling to show up for my child in the way I need to."

2. ANGER

Anger is another highly complex emotional state that may also be viewed as an escalation of frustration. When dysregulated parents feel angry about their own dysregulated states, they may feel a strong urge to confront the problem or source of anger. However, because the source of the problem is their own limited capacity for self-regulation, this anger often becomes internalized and directed at the self, which can feel negative and unhealthy.

The internalized belief often associated with anger for dysregulated parents is one of injustice, unfairness, and betrayal and might sound something like "I have violated the rules." This belief implies that there is a standard or precedent that the parent hopes to fulfill but instead feel they continue to violate in some manner. For example:

"I get really mad at myself, like a deep anger for having these feelings when becoming a parent is something I longed for."

3. INADEQUACY

The sense of inadequacy that dysregulated parents frequently feel conveys a sense of insufficiency, self-doubt, or the feeling of "not measuring up" to the parenting standard or expectations that have been established. This inadequacy can also feel like inferiority or incompetence, which can be really uncomfortable, especially when you're in the thick of a tough parenting moment.

Inadequacy for dysregulated parents often turns into an internalized belief of "I am not good enough" or "I am a failure." Not only can this inadequacy linger, but it can also lead to a host of other distressing mental health concerns, such as anxiety and depression. Here's one parent's take on their own sense of inadequacy because of dysregulation:

"I feel like a failure for repeating behaviors exhibited in my childhood that I know I don't want to repeat. I just can't seem to get it right."

4. DOUBT

The feeling of doubt or second-guessing your parenting is a common experience, especially among those parents who find themselves chronically dysregulated. Doubtfulness was a major feeling that parents described in reaction to their inability to self-regulate in the moments it matters most. This sense of doubt involves a deep uncertainty or skepticism about one's own parenting ability and can lead to hesitation, indecisiveness, and a huge lack of confidence.

The internalized belief associated with this doubtfulness tends to be "I am unsure," leading parents to doubt and second-guess their parenting decisions, approach, ability, and effectiveness. One parent captured this perfectly:

"I'm always doubtful in my ability to parent. It's a feeling of 'I don't know what I'm doing' and doesn't seem to go away."

5. LONELINESS

Did you know that parents who often feel dysregulated may then feel more lonely as a result? The parents I spoke to describe a deep sense of isolation, emotional disconnection, and general feeling of being alone as a result of chronic dysregulation. Why? Many of them were afraid to admit that they were struggling at this level. Feeling guilty and fearing shame (both emotions that we will soon discuss), they instead decided to keep this issue to themselves and began to believe that "I must be the only one."

Parental loneliness can feel like a pervasive emptiness, even in the presence of others. Many times, parents long for opportunities to be open and honest about all that they are challenged with, without the judgment that often accompanies this reality. They often begin to internalize the belief that "I am the only one." They begin to believe that there are no others experiencing the same feelings or challenges, and therefore, there must be something wrong with them. However, we know that is far from the truth. For example:

"When I am having trouble controlling myself, I feel this internal loneliness and isolation. Honestly, it's because I'm afraid to be judged and just feeling really ashamed."

6. SADNESS

The feeling of sadness often goes unnoticed or unacknowledged once we become parents. As a society, we tend to dismiss this common and important emotion, assuming that it's something we mostly are responsible for supporting our children through. However, the reality is that adults and parents alike feel sadness, and fairly often. Parents reported this sadness seems to be related to a negative perspective they have developed about themselves as a result of being so chronically dysregulated.

Sadness is another complex emotion that can be associated with several internalized beliefs regarding dysregulated parenting, including "I am helpless" (implying that they cannot be helped and things will not get better), "I am powerless" (implying that they do not have the power to change the situation), and "I am unlovable" (meaning, they have made so many mistakes that they now are undeserving of love). Here is how one parent described this:

"I often feel lots of sadness, because of feelings of being a bad mom and a bad example."

7. ENVY

Parenting today means being privy to so much information about the ways in which others are parenting. Social media has made it so that we are able to peek into the lives of others and get a sense of how they live and what their own relationships might be like with their children. This experience doesn't only occur only on the internet, as we often tend to interpret and develop ideas or opinions of other parents we may meet in our daily lives as well. However, this comes with a downside and is inevitably how envy comes to be.

The internalized belief associated with envy for dysregulated parents is "I want what they have" and implies that someone else has the situation, circumstance, abilities, or relationships they desire. This often includes a desire for self-composure, the ability to self-regulate, or a general desire to be a "better parent." For example:

"I feel envious of those who are able to 'regulate' themselves better. I want to be able to do that too but I can't."

8. JUDGMENT

Judgment involves the act of forming an opinion or evaluation about something or someone based on a personal standard, belief, or observation. An unfortunate truth of becoming a parent is that you will be judged and you also may judge someone else. This sense of perceived judgment from others regarding parenting has been spoken about for generations, with parents often keenly protecting themselves from any judgment that they may receive from friends, family members, or the general public.

The internalized belief associated with judgment for dysregulated parents is "Other people think I am bad." This belief reflects a persistent expectation that other people may perceive or interpret one's own parenting approach or abilities to be flawed, wrong, ineffective, or simply put—bad. Here's how one parent explained it:

"I'm constantly feeling judged by others about how I parent, even if they haven't said anything to me about it."

9. GUILT

Have you ever said or done the wrong thing with your kids? If so, I'm sure you are very familiar with this next feeling. Guilt is an emotional state that, unfortunately, is all too common to parents, especially those struggling with chronic dysregulation. The reality of parenting is that we will often make mistakes; however, some of us then go on to feel the heavy and burdensome nature that guilt brings. Unresolved guilt can eventually lead to self-blame, sadness, shame, and even anxiety.

Dysregulated parents who constantly feel guilt regarding their inability to self-regulate begin to internalize the belief that "I did something bad." This belief becomes pervasive within their parenting experience and doesn't allow them to move forward or grow from the dysregulating experience so that they may learn differently. Here is how one parent explained their guilt:

"I feel guilty because I am raising my child differently than how I want or imagined. I feel like a failure and then guilty for having those feelings. I just don't know what I'm doing."

10. SHAME

I intentionally saved shame for last because it seems to be the most consistent emotional state that parents shared about. When parents are chronically dysregulated and don't feel able to self-regulate, the majority of them feel shame. Shame is a powerful and painful emotional state that arises from the perception of our own shortcomings or inadequacies. It is accompanied by a profound sense of embarrassment and humiliation, and a deep desire to hide or withdraw.

Shame typically involves persistent negative self-evaluations and beliefs about our own character, actions, and parenting abilities. Therefore, the internalized belief that is commonly associated with shame for dysregulated parents is "I am bad." This belief is so simple and yet can be so devastating to one's well-being as a parent, confidence, and also relationship with one's children. Here's one example of how shame plays out:

"I am so ashamed to even be having these feelings and challenges, especially when being a parent is something I've longed for. I just feel lots of shame for not being able to set an example for my kids on how to use regulation tools when I'm overwhelmed."

EMOTIONAL STATE	INTERNALIZED BELIEF FOR DYSREGULATED PARENTS
Frustration	I am not effective.
Anger	I have violated the rules.
Inadequacy	I am not good enough.
Doubt	I am unsure.
Loneliness	I am the only one.

EMOTIONAL STATE	INTERNALIZED BELIEF FOR DYSREGULATED PARENTS
Sadness	I am helpless/powerless/unlovable.
Envy	I want what they have.
Judgment	Other people think I am bad.
Guilt	I did something bad.
Shame	I am bad.

CHAPTER 9

The Five Big Concerns About Dysregulation

Five big concerns tend to occur for parents around the meaning and impact of their dysregulation, and I want to share them with you. However, rather than providing a direct solution for the concerns, I am going to do something a little different from what you may be expecting. I understand the desire to know what to do and how to solve your concerns, but I also know that further consideration for how to think about the concerns can be more helpful.

Don't worry, I will be providing tangible solutions in the next part of this book, but this chapter will be the foundation for consideration you need to more deeply apply any strategies that are offered later. So let's take a moment to delve into the five big concerns of dysregulated parents.

1. AM I INADEQUATE AS A PARENT?

This concern is often linked with fear and a sense of inadequacy that can lead to isolation because of wanting to hide the perceived inadequacy, and also worry over criticism or judgment from others. Some of the parents from our study put it this way:

"I'm concerned that I'm inadequate as a parent quite often. Did I say or do the 'right' thing? Am I being the best father I can be?"

"I feel like I don't do [self-regulation] well enough and often-times find myself exploding or completely shutting down, which I feel really guilty about. I don't want to have to leave all the time to calm myself down because I don't want my girls thinking or feeling neglected. When I can't self-regulate I'm not parenting well and worry that my girls will not be able to successfully regulate themselves either."

"My toddler has developmental delays, so it's hard to determine what's typical toddler behavior and what's happening as a result of the delay. That may always be a challenge for me. I worry about how to support him best when he's having a meltdown, and how to make sure I'm self-regulating when he's overstimulated or tired or frustrated. It makes me wonder if I have what it takes to do all this."

"The intense rage that surfaces so quickly now as a mom causes me to not recognize myself and makes me question my ability and worthiness as a mom."

Your biggest fear may be that you are inadequate as a parent and—because you are inadequate—you may cause harm or not properly equip your child with the tools they need to navigate the world around them. However, instead of believing that you are inadequate, I challenge you to understand that as a parent, every moment with your child is a learning opportunity. Even the mistakes and mishaps are there to teach you more about your child and yourself. Therefore, you are not inadequate. Instead, you are learning to navigate a world that often feels overwhelming, tiresome, and full of high demands. You are learning more and more every day and have grown far more than you realize.

2. AM I SETTING A BAD EXAMPLE FOR SELF-REGULATION FOR MY KIDS?

This concern can also be linked to that feeling of inadequacy as a parent, as well as a sense of guilt for the belief that "I am doing something bad." Unaddressed feelings of inadequacy and guilt can quickly lead to hopelessness, depression, and other grave mental health concerns. Parents relayed the following about setting bad examples:

"I"m worried about the impact my dysregulation has on my kids' emotional well-being."

"I'm setting a bad example when I snap and feel guilt if I give myself a time-out. Also, the tools I use don't seem to sustain me."

"My concerns are that I am impacting my daughter's ability to self-regulate and not setting an ideal parenting example."

"I want to be a model for self-regulation so my child knows how to do it as he gets older, but I really don't think that is happening now."

"I'm concerned that my children are dysregulated because I can't consistently model self-control."

You may fear that your children will learn bad habits and negative ways of coping with their own challenges as a result of your bad example. But what if you are not setting a bad example at all? What if, instead, you are showing your children that you are human, and so are they? I urge you to see that as a parent, it is okay to make mistakes and even more important for your children to see you making mistakes. This normalizes the process of learning and helps them to have compassion for themselves when they make mistakes too. So, no, you are not setting a bad example, but instead are demonstrating the beauty in humanity and what it means to have compassion for yourself in the process.

3. AM I REPEATING A PATTERN OF PARENTING THAT I GREW UP WITH?

I've found this concern to be very common among the millennial generation, as they are embracing a new set of parenting standards that more greatly emphasize the emotional and psychological well-being of their children. This concern can be associated with a fear of judgment from others, as many are attempting to shift the norms and narratives of parenting and can become critical of themselves and others in the process. That can easily lead to loneliness and isolation in an attempt to protect and hide one's self from judgment and criticism from others. Many of the parents from our study have had this experience and shared it this way:

"My mom used to blow up on me a lot as a kid so I worry I can leave the same emotional wounds on my child."

"I don't want my kid to feel like she's an inconvenience. I felt like that a lot when I was a kid. When I don't self-regulate, I'm pretty sure she feels that way."

"I am concerned about all the times I struggle with my ability to self-regulate. I want to put my daughter in a position to be able to self-regulate better than I can. I find myself trying to parent differently than my parents did and so my concerns tend to arise when I see myself struggle to meet those goals."

"I struggle with reminding myself that it's okay to pause and instead find myself repeating unwanted patterns that I grew up seeing in my own parents' behaviors."

"My biggest fear is that I will become like my father. He loved us dearly but he was so explosive when he became upset and it scared me. Now whenever I yell or get upset I get so worried that I've just re-created a moment similar to what I experienced with him."

You fear repeating a pattern of parenting that you dislike and that you may become just like the parent that you've always feared, resented, or now have complicated feelings for because of how they parented you. However, what if you're not repeating that pattern at all? Could you instead see that you are working through a courageous process of unlearning that can take years? Many people are unable to break generational cycles because it's difficult, and yet, you are still choosing to work through yours every single day. Therefore, you are not repeating a pattern of broken parenting. Instead, you have committed to a lifelong process that is challenging and has already begun to pay off. Your children have already benefited from your commitment to create a new parenting normal, and they will continue to benefit because you are choosing to do something different.

4. HOW WILL I EVER LEARN TO SELF-REGULATE WHEN TIMES ARE ALWAYS HARD?

Parenting is extremely challenging, and the parents who hold this concern have realized that this challenge seems to persist, despite changes that may come. This concern is frequently linked with a feeling of anxiety regarding the future and one's capacity as a parent. For these parents, it can feel as if the future will continue to bring more issues and concerns, and that can also bring fear. Here's how some of the parents from our study explained this:

"I often think about the extent to which I struggle in parenting but not as much in other relational settings. I'm not sure if it will ever get better."

"I'm concerned that life is going to continue to be difficult and that I won't have the ability to regulate myself the way I need in order to be the best parent for my kids. We all need for me to be the best version of myself. I know that looks different at different times but I'm concerned that when I go through hard times, I'm going to be a crappy mom."

"I'm concerned that I don't actually have the capacity to self-regulate more than I have because of the stressors I have not yet eliminated."

"My patience can get really thin very quickly. I can get frustrated and overstimulated quickly, causing my approach to be a little louder and not conducive to talking to the children in a low, kind tone. I'm just worried that with everything going on, that won't change anytime soon."

"I'm worried that I've forgotten how to self-regulate and I'll never learn how or be able to implement any strategies."

You fear you will never be able to self-regulate consistently because life will always have its challenges, and because life can feel so daunting, you may always struggle with the same pattern and cycles of dysregulation. However, instead of believing this, what if you soon realized that while life will definitely always have its challenges, you are capable of picking up new strategies and tools to manage the difficulties along the way? Instead of focusing on the hard times and the negative outcomes, what if you shifted your focus to every new skill that you might develop with each difficult time, including the difficulties that come in parenting? This can be the case for you when it comes to how you begin to learn new ways to self-regulate and manage your own big feelings. I know that you have the capacity to grow, learn, and develop new skills that will continue to benefit you in the hard times that are sure to come your way.

5. WILL MY DYSREGULATION CAUSE A LASTING NEGATIVE IMPACT ON THE RELATIONSHIP WITH MY FAMILY OR THEIR MENTAL HEALTH?

While this may have been the last concern, it definitely was not the least pressing. A significant number of parents from our study expressed concern and fear regarding this potential negative impact on their family, especially their children. This concern can contribute to a number of emotional states, including inadequacy, fear, sadness, guilt, and shame. Parents from our study expressed this as such:

"I do not want to damage my children because I can't get myself together. That scares me."

"My concern is that I can cause permanent damage to his confidence and personality and that he will learn bad habits from me."

"I'm worried that if I don't get it together, I'll mess my kids up. I'm generally cranky and no one wants to be around that."

"I don't like being an angry parent who shouts. I worry that my children will have a negative experience of my emotional dysregulation and the cycle will continue in them. I don't want my stress and anxiety to have big effects on them."

"I'm concerned that my children are being traumatized by my inability to self-regulate because I can't regulate them either."

You fear that every time you lose control and succumb to your dysregulated state, you are hurting your family. You worry you will yell, scream, snap, or become irritated with your children one too many times and it will permanently damage the relationship and bond you've worked so hard to cultivate with them. However, you are bigger and much greater than your mistakes. Additionally, while ruptures in relationships can hurt (especially those ruptures with our children), repair matters so much more and has the power to heal any rupture that may have occurred. Remember that in parenthood, you will make mistakes, even after you've read this entire book front to back, ten times over. You will continue to mess up or say the wrong things because you are human, and that doesn't inherently harm your children. Rather, the disinterest in repair and lack of accountability is what can cause long-term damage. Your effort to understand yourself and do something different, especially by using this book as a tool, is an indication that you want to change and that your relationship with your children matters greatly. Therefore, less focus on the mistakes and huge emphasis on the repair. How can you acknowledge what has happened, repair the hurt feelings, and move on even better? I trust and believe that you are capable of that beautiful reality.

PART III

From Dysregulated to Regulated: A Method for Change

・・・

CHAPTER 10

The PCR Method for Dysregulated Parents

Remember the plunger?

I'm happy to report that my child has not played with the plunger ever since the day I completely lost it when I found him doing that very thing in our bathroom. I'm thrilled that we aren't having to worry about that issue anymore, but the memory of that day still bothers me.

After seeing my therapist and gaining the realization about being dysregulated, with several factors, circumstances, or issues that led to me feeling that way, I began to think deeply about what had actually happened in that bathroom. After I apologized and managed to repair things with my son, and everything seemingly "went back to normal," I continued to reflect on what my days, nights, and time in general looked and felt like at this point as a parent. I made sure to give myself space to cool down and be able to process everything that came to mind to me about that very moment.

You know what continued to play in my head? It was the look of fear on his face. The look of fear that he felt as I yelled so loudly and continuously kept replaying in my head, over and over and over again. I never wanted my children to feel afraid as a result of my reactions and yet, it had happened. I soon began to feel deeply ashamed, guilty, and fearful of whether we could actually move past this. Or rather, whether I could actually move past this. Would it be possible for me to figure out how to control my anger, temper, anxiety, and big emotions, or generally stay regulated enough to be the parent I truly want to be?

I also started to realize that my big reaction to him playing with the plunger that day didn't even teach him anything about the plunger or proper care when going to the bathroom. Nothing about how I reacted that day had helped him to understand why it wasn't a good idea to play with plungers or even what the plunger is actually used for. Very little about how I reacted that day helped him learn, grow, or feel supported in our relationship. For me, that felt like a big failure.

Those few days of deep reflection about this incident helped me understand that my reaction to him, with the plunger, had very little to do with my son or what may have been going on in the bathroom that day. I now understand that, instead, it was so many other things that had been adding up along the way to trigger that very moment. It was my own lack of awareness of what was really affecting me that led to an unreasonable and overly exaggerated reaction that unfortunately scared my child. It was my prolonged dysregulated state, my limited awareness of it, and my lack of skills for how to recover from being so dysregulated. In that moment, I did not have the capacity and ability to regulate myself. That newfound awareness, understanding, and the steps I took afterward were just the start of how I began to turn this all around.

Today, it feels like I've been given a second chance. I am fully embracing this new opportunity to get things right as a parent and with my children. I'm also fully embracing and so grateful for this opportunity to share what I've learned with you, so you, too, can begin to enjoy and celebrate your second chance. Because what I know all too well is that none of this has been or will be easy, and to be honest, a few years of deep reflection and immense effort at change still haven't made me an expert. However, I'm much further than I was that day with the plunger and so excited to share the practical, conscious, and very realistic approaches that finally began to make sense for me. I'm on my way and I know you will be too.

INTRODUCING THE PCR METHOD FOR DYSREGULATED PARENTS

I'm so excited to finally introduce to you the PCR (Practical, Realistic, Conscious) Method for Dysregulated Parents.

The makings of the PCR Method has been a journey. All through the process of developing the Self-Regulation in Parenting Research Study, gathering participants who would be a good fit for the study, conducting the actual research, speaking directly to parents for interviews, and then also writing this book, the big question that constantly remained in my mind was this: What exactly will help these parents who have struggled with dysregulation for far too long get from point A to point B?

Point A is a place where you are ready for change. You've been looking for answers for a long time about how to resolve what you've been feeling and have been left frustrated and alone.

You haven't been getting the experience of joy in parenthood that you originally thought you would, and the feelings of guilt and shame are taking their toll.

Point B is exactly where you are headed now. With the help of the PCR Method, you will finally know your triggers for dysregulation. You'll feel confident and comfortable in your parenting, having capacity for self-regulation on a consistent basis. You'll be able to model healthy regulation for your children, feeling much closer and more connected in relationship to them. You will finally be able to gain control of the guilt and shame that have been haunting you for far too long, being able to truly experience the joy you've always imagined.

What I love most about the PCR Method is that it acknowledges that there is no "one-size fits all." Yes, while many of us are having very similar experiences as we struggle to gain skills and capacity for self-regulation, we may still have very different needs when it comes to how that gets done. It is also the case that at any given moment, you may need something different than what worked a day ago, a month ago, or even a few minutes ago.

You are ever-evolving, especially in parenthood. Each moment brings new challenges, which is why the PCR Method contains three separate approaches, which will better help you manage and address any and every need that you may have on your journey to better self-regulation.

This method is simple: At any given moment when you are feeling dysregulated or simply have a desire to strengthen skills or capacity for self-regulation, pick an approach to practice. There will be moments when one approach feels more aligned with you and your needs than the others, and that is to be expected. However, over time you'll realize that it is the combined practice of all three approaches that will help you feel fully equipped with the self-regulation skills and strategies to manage every aspect of parenthood.

Each approach within the PCR Method is important and there is no pressure to practice each one at every moment during which you are dysregulated. Follow your instinct to help you know which approach is best for you when you need one.

For now, here's a brief overview of each approach of the PCR Method. You will get a much deeper dive into each in the coming chapters.

1. THE PRACTICAL APPROACH

The Practical Approach is referred to as such because it is the most common style of intervention one would expect if they were to seek help for chronic dysregulation from a psychologist or other mental health provider. This approach is the most hands-on set of strategies within the PCR Method and requires you to really take a moment to identify what has actually gone on within the previous four weeks, how the events and circumstances of those four weeks have affected you, and what to do about it.

The approach requires sitting down and doing some homework. Because of that, it may remind you of school or doing an assignment, but it's well worth your while.

The Practical Approach will be extremely valuable for you because it will ask you to reflect, identify, practice, develop, and implement strategies that we often don't have the time to consider in a typical day. More specifically, the Practice Approach consists of a six-step system, asking you to complete the following:

1. **Pause and Reflect**

2. **Identify Your Triggers**

3. **Practice Recognizing Your Triggers**

4. **Develop Your Trigger Support Plan**

5. **Implement Your Trigger Support Plan**

6. **Edit and Revise Your Plan**

After learning about the six steps of the Practical Approach (see page 125), you should have every practical and tangible tool you need for going from chronic dysregulation to manageable self-regulation.

2. THE CONSCIOUS APPROACH

The second approach within the PCR Method is the Conscious Approach. This approach may remind you of conscious-parenting style (page 42), because several of their principles align. Both emphasize self-awareness, presence, and intentionality when it comes to parenting. Therefore, this approach will feel different from the Practical Approach because it's designed to help you slow down and go much deeper. It emphasizes skill development, as well as looking into the underlying motives, emotions, and experiences that are at the foundations of your actions and reactions.

The Conscious Approach will help you to focus on fostering a deeper connection with not only your child, but also yourself. This approach will cultivate an inner state that better allows for emotional and psychological well-being for both you and your family. We will do this by reviewing the following four aspects of this approach:

- **Alignment with conscious-parenting.** We will review the most important principles of conscious-parenting that better serve your ability and capacity for self-regulation.
- **Active engagement in re-parenting.** You will learn all about re-parenting and how actively engaging in the process will help restore your mind, body, and psychological well-being following months or even years of dysregulation.
- **The conscious takeaway.** You will gain an excellent takeaway for why it's important to be able to self-regulate and how to get back to it if you've lost motivation for it.
- **The ultimate goal.** You will learn what that ultimate goal is and the #1 reflection question to help you stay grounded in this goal. In your biggest and most challenging parenting moments, you will be able to come back to the ultimate goal of the Conscious Approach, which will also ensure that you remain connected to yourself, your children, and your long-lasting ability to regulate in the future.

3. THE REALIST APPROACH

The third and final approach within the PCR Method is the Realist Approach, which asks you to be as realistic as possible about your destiny and experience as a parent. Part of that realistic ask is really learning how to accept some of the hard truths of what this reality now brings. A major truth that we will address and learn how to accept is the fact that dysregulation as a parent will happen.

You may be asking, "Wait, isn't this book supposed to help me not become dysregulated? So how is it now that we are saying that dysregulation will happen?"

As a psychologist, this is one of my favorite conundrums to address. The most common expectation is that the issue or concern that clients came to me with will be all but eliminated by the end of our work together. People often expect that if they work hard to address an issue or concern, that means it will completely go away. That, unfortunately, is not true.

Yes, working with a therapist can help to minimize and decrease the presence and effect of these issues and concerns; however, the work comes in when you learn how to begin living with a little bit of those issues and concerns. Similarly, this book has likely already helped you to better identify when you're dysregulated and understand all that affects you throughout your day that probably leads to dysregulation, and the rest of the book will give you even more personalized strategies for continuing to manage all of this. And yet, dysregulation will continue to show up in your life.

This is parenting. This is life.

The Realist Approach will help you to understand how to implement "radical acceptance" into your experience as you work to combat dysregulation. This approach will acknowledge all the things that have changed since you became a parent and what it means to accept these changes, even when you don't like them. The Realist Approach will give you more insight into the fears that serve as barriers to your acceptance process, and what to do about them. Last, the approach will provide you with some affirmations that you can carry along on your journey.

PUTTING IT ALL TOGETHER

Now is the time to put it all together and prepare for what life will look and feel like on the other side of chronic dysregulation. The Practical, Conscious, and Realistic Approaches come together to create a method that you can use at every moment of your parenting journey—one that will evolve with you as time passes. There may be one approach you gravitate toward more than another, and that's okay. You'll also likely notice that next year, that same method may feel different and you'll be more drawn to one of the other approaches. That is also okay.

What I want most for you is to remain open to the possibilities of where this will take you and also to follow your instincts about what you need.

Let's go.

CHAPTER 11

• • •

The Practical Approach

Close your eyes for a moment and imagine this: Think back to one of your worst parenting moments—the one that continues to replay in your head over and over again, that made you feel the most guilt you've ever felt, for weeks or months at a time. It is one that you've probably never shared with anyone because the guilt and shame you felt about the event kept you wanting to hide it instead. You fear that you had either harmed your child's psychological development for good or had finally turned into your own parent, which probably has been something you've never wanted.

Fully imagine that moment right now, recalling what happened, how it felt, how you felt, and what you imagine your child felt. I want you to feel everything that comes up as you have this in mind.

Now, you're probably wondering why I would torture you with remembering your worst parenting moment when you've been struggling to move past it for weeks, months, or even years now. Well, trust me, I have a few reasons.

First, just as you've read this paragraph and imagined your worst parenting moment, so have hundreds or thousands of other parents who are reading this too. I would bet that no one who read that paragraph said to themselves, "Hmm, I actually don't have a 'worst parenting moment' to imagine." We all have had one. Of course, all the moments imagined are probably very different from each other because we all have such varied experiences. However, one thing we all have in common is that we are not always our best selves, especially when it comes to parenting.

Second, and more importantly, I want to help prepare you for the first approach of the PCR Method, the Practical Approach. Yes, you could probably read about this approach and imagine how to apply these interventions when the time comes, but I want you to be able to read through this entire approach having held one specific parenting moment in mind, so that you are able to really understand and apply all that you'll learn to it. Meanwhile, it's also possible that there is another tough parenting moment that has happened more recently, or as you're reading the chapter, one may come up. Feel free to apply this approach and all its interventions to those moments too. But understand that if you can apply it to the worst, you'll be able to apply it to all the other hard moments that are sure to come.

THE PRACTICAL APPROACH: A SIX-STEP SYSTEM

The goal of the Practical Approach is to help you better identify triggers and other factors that contribute to your dysregulated state. With the help of the Practical Approach, you'll also describe and understand how these triggers and factors affect your physical, mental, and emotional health. You'll gain a very good understanding of how all this impacts your parenting and capacity for self-regulation. Furthermore, once you are able to identify these triggers and dysregulating factors around you, you'll be able to cope and manage them a lot faster than you've been able to in the past.

As you begin to implement the six-step system of the Practical Approach, understand that this system needs time. (I'll clearly indicate how much time I believe you should spend on each step of the system.) As you become more familiar with this system, it seems reasonable to believe that you'll be able to move through each step faster or more efficiently. However, please go slowly and take your time during the initial rounds.

STEP 1: PAUSE AND REFLECT

Time: 3 to 5 days

How many times have you had a tough parenting moment brought on by dysregulation and immediately tried to "fix it"? This may have been in the form of an apology or immediately trying to find books to read for how to better manage your anger or overstimulation. Or perhaps, your guilt and shame immediately took over, leaving you incapable of solutions because your feelings felt so intense. The all-consuming "I'm a bad parent" belief took over and then you started to overcompensate for your mistake in other ways that eventually also ended up backfiring.

I know this cycle and today I want you to break it. Immediately after having a moment (or season) like this, it's most helpful to pause and reflect. The big question I want you to ask yourself at this moment is "What happened?"

You may be wondering why this step needs three to five days to complete, and it's because I've found that parents have a really hard time with pausing and reflecting. There are often so many distractions and other responsibilities that impede our ability to really stop and think more deeply. On the flip side, I do not believe it to be helpful to spend more than five days on this task. I want you to reflect, not ruminate, which could lead you to get stuck in the cycles of guilt, shame, and a host of other difficult emotions.

As a busy parent, pausing to reflect realistically might look like:

- Writing down the phrase "What happened?" on a sticky note and putting it on your mirror, so that it reminds you to continue reflecting as you go throughout your day.
- Taking an extra few minutes in the bathroom to check in with yourself about how you're feeling following that tough moment (I promise the kids won't know you're hiding out).
- Spending a few extra minutes during your lunch break to reflect on the tough moment.
- Putting on some noise-canceling headphones and pondering the tough moment as you cook dinner or straighten up.
- Zoning out to your thoughts about the tough moment during your morning or evening drive to and from work or school.

Here are some questions it will be most helpful to pause and reflect on:

1. What happened? Simply replay the tough parenting moment in your mind, trying to be as objective as possible.

2. What was I feeling at that moment? Try to pull for any feeling word that comes to mind.

3. What feeling was I feeling right before the tough moment?

4. How did I feel after that moment?

5. What was my child trying to communicate or achieve in that moment (if applicable)?

6. What was the outcome of this tough moment? For me? For my child? For the family?

7. How does this align with my vision and goals for parenting?

8. Where do I want to go from here?

9. How can I give myself grace and compassion in this moment?

10. How can I affirm my strengths and abilities as a parent at this moment?

STEP 2: IDENTIFY YOUR TRIGGERS

Time: 1 to 2 days

After you've taken time to reflect about what actually happened for you during that tough moment, you'll likely be feeling more relaxed and finally ready to begin the early stages of seeking a solution. You may still feel some guilt, shame, or remorse, but the feelings are likely less urgent and more manageable (if not, please spend a bit more time in step 1). Now, it's time to identify the triggers that lead up to the tough parenting moment in the first place.

"Identify your triggers" has become a very common phrase, but even with dysregulation, it's important to be able to identify the triggers that contribute to it. On the surface, it may seem like the reasons why you became dysregulated or had a tough parenting moment may be because of something that occurred in that moment; however, often with deeper discovery, you'll find that there were a host of other issues or factors that led to the dysregulation.

A "trigger" is simply a stimulus, event, situation, or condition that elicits a reaction. With that definition, you can probably imagine that literally anything can become a trigger depending on the circumstances. So for this step, consider all the things that may have gradually contributed to the reaction you had at that moment.

Additionally, stretch yourself to think through the triggers that may have been present in the previous four weeks that led up to the tough moment. This will help you to get past what's on the surface and really begin to address all that falls much deeper below the surface of dysregulation.

I recommend you spend one to two days on this step. It will likely require more focused and intentional energy and you may have to plan a moment to sit down and thoroughly think through all the factors that likely contributed to that tough parenting moment you experienced. Consider setting a timer for thirty to sixty minutes to comb through your calendar, helping you to remember events or situations that may have occurred in the past four weeks. Feel free to plan another thirty to sixty minutes the next day to finish the task, if needed.

Below is a chart that you can use to identify your triggers. I've included some common life categories that may involve certain triggers. Feel free to add in unique categories that may apply to your life. Simply fill in the boxes with "triggers" you identify for each corresponding week and category.

MY DYSREGULATION TRIGGERS

	WEEK 1	WEEK 2
HOME		
WORK		
KIDS		
MARRIAGE/ PARTNERSHIPS		
FINANCES		
HEALTH		
OTHER RELATIONSHIPS		
OTHER		
OTHER		

MY DYSREGULATION TRIGGERS

WEEK 3	WEEK 4	
		HOME
		WORK
		KIDS
		MARRIAGE/ PARTNERSHIPS
		FINANCES
		HEALTH
		OTHER RELATIONSHIP
		OTHER
		OTHER

STEP 3: PRACTICE RECOGNIZING YOUR TRIGGERS

Time: 2 to 3 weeks

Before moving into a plan to actually manage your triggers, you first need to practice recognizing when the triggers occur. Recognizing our triggers is often an overlooked and under-developed skill that leads to dysregulation because it simply takes us too long to realize when things are happening to us or that we are being affected by triggers. Therefore, being able to recognize when your triggers are present is crucial and will help prevent an ongoing or recurrent cycle of dysregulation.

The goal and instructions for this step are simple: Take two to three weeks to practice recognizing when any of your triggers are present. Scan for any of the triggers you identify in step 2 with the help of your triggers chart. Likewise, scan for and recognize additional triggers that may be new or unique to this current period of time.

For some, it may be possible to complete this step passively by keeping it in mind throughout your day and quietly letting yourself know when you've recognized a trigger. You may want to write out "Find your triggers" on a sticky note to keep with you during the day or set a few reminders on your phone, gently asking you to check in on the trigger hunting. Others may need a more structured approach, and if that's the case, it's fine to use a blank copy of the trigger chart to plot out triggers you find or recognize in the coming two to three weeks.

After completing this step, you should notice that you are able to identify when triggers occur, faster and more consistently.

Once you begin to notice this is happening for you, you will be ready to move onto step 4.

STEP 4: DEVELOP YOUR TRIGGER SUPPORT PLAN

Time: 2 to 3 days

Once you learn how to actually recognize your triggers, it's time to develop your trigger coping plan. This step will ask you to get really creative as you consider how it would be best for you to cope with, manage, or solve the triggers that you've worked hard to recognize in your environment.

As you go through this process, first decide whether the trigger will receive a plan that provides *coping, managing,* or *solving.* Let's take a moment to differentiate between these terms:

Coping: Living with this trigger (even if the trigger remains unchanged).

Managing: Keeping this trigger controlled or preventing it from getting worse.

Solving: Fixing or completely eliminating this trigger.

Below is a chart that you can use to develop your trigger support plan. I recommend selecting your top ten most dysregulating or most frequently occurring triggers to add to this chart. For each trigger, determine your plan type—cope with, manage, or solve the trigger. Finally, indicate what strategy you will use to provide yourself with support for this trigger (how you plan to implement, cope, or solve this trigger).

TRIGGER	PLAN TYPE	TRIGGER COPING STRATEGY
1.	☐ Cope ☐ Manage ☐ Solve	
2.	☐ Cope ☐ Manage ☐ Solve	
3.	☐ Cope ☐ Manage ☐ Solve	
4.	☐ Cope ☐ Manage ☐ Solve	
5.	☐ Cope ☐ Manage ☐ Solve	
6.	☐ Cope ☐ Manage ☐ Solve	
7.	☐ Cope ☐ Manage ☐ Solve	
8.	☐ Cope ☐ Manage ☐ Solve	

TRIGGER	PLAN TYPE	TRIGGER COPING STRATEGY
9.	☐ Cope ☐ Manage ☐ Solve	
10.	☐ Cope ☐ Manage ☐ Solve	

STEP 5: IMPLEMENT YOUR TRIGGER SUPPORT PLAN
Time: 3 Weeks

We've all heard the saying that it takes twenty-one days to form a new habit. While I don't believe there is scientific evidence to truly support this, I do believe the saying helps to remind us that new habits take time. Therefore, I want you to take at least three weeks to fully implement your trigger support plan for step 5. Step 4 required you to actually create the plan, and now step 5 is asking you to go make the plan happen.

As you go through your day-to-day, continue to focus on recognizing when your triggers are present. Once you recognize one of your top ten triggers occurring, your goal is to implement the strategy that you identified for supporting yourself through this trigger.

Simply put, go and set your plan into place, giving yourself grace as you gradually make it a consistent routine.

STEP 6: EDIT AND REVISE YOUR PLAN

Time: Ongoing

Every plan needs to be edited and revised, because nothing stays the same for too long. This same idea will apply to the plan you've created. In order to ensure that your dysregulation is managed for the foreseeable future, I recommend taking time to edit and revise your plan every three months. This may look like:

- Going back to step 5 and reimplementing your trigger management plan. It's possible that your routines have changed and your plan needs to fit a new set of habits or changed lifestyle.

- Checking in to review the plan you developed in step 4 to see if the coping strategies are still working for your triggers.

- Going back to step 3 and practicing the ability to recognize triggers once again, because it's possible that you need a refresher for quickly realizing when triggers are occurring.

- Redoing step 2, this time to identify triggers that better align with any recent changes that may have occurred in the last few months.

- Completely starting the entire Practical Approach fresh at step 1, because sometimes we need a complete restart.

Whatever your edit and revision look like, just know that change is okay and to be expected. I hope you are able to embrace whatever may come with it.

CHAPTER 12

The Conscious Approach

In 2021, I read a book called *The Conscious Parent.* At the time, I was two years into motherhood and had a two-year-old and an infant who was probably close to two or three months old. Those days with a young toddler and brand-new baby were so hard. I had been lucky to feel as though one baby was "manageable" and recall some really good times, but then came the second and I began to question everything.

"I know we wanted them to be close in age, but did we make a mistake by not waiting longer?"

That was a question I constantly asked my husband and also silently wondered to myself, because the chaos and overstimulation brought on by these two little people felt immensely tiring. It wasn't long before I began to struggle with postpartum anxiety. I was also juggling the grief that came with the recent loss of my father. I was in awe of how much "life stuff" was going on while I was simply trying to recover from a second C-section and cope with being a mom of two very little children.

How dare life not stop so that I can actually be present to soak all of this in? How the hell was I actually supposed to recover and not lose my mind when there was so much to think about, so much to process, and so much to feel sad and anxious over?

It must have been divine timing to have the words and voice of Dr. Shefali Tsabary come through my headphones via audiobook. I was new to her work and somehow, her book about conscious-parenting really aligned with where I was at that moment. It was a huge reminder that even in the chaos of that time, I could go deeper into understanding what was happening, how it was affecting me, and what that meant for how I would show up as a parent. In those tough moments, I received the insight that I needed to slow down, tune in, and become a lot more mindful of how I reacted and responded to my young children. That insight has continued to feel like a gift that keeps on giving.

THE CONSCIOUS APPROACH

The goal of the Conscious Approach is to help you slow down and go deeper into your journey of understanding what contributes to your dysregulated state. With the help of the Conscious Approach, you'll be able to truly focus on self-awareness, presence, and intentionality as a parent. You'll also develop a very good understanding of the underlying motives, emotions, and experiences that are at the core of your daily actions and reactions.

I'm excited for the Conscious Approach to help you develop a deeper connection with not only your child, but also yourself. In order to make this happen, we will focus on four important aspects of this approach: alignment with conscious-parenting, active engagement in re-parenting, the conscious takeaway, and the ultimate goal.

ALIGNMENT WITH CONSCIOUS-PARENTING

If this topic feels familiar, it may partly be because we discussed key strategies and characteristics of conscious-parenting when we explored a variety of parenting practices in chapter 2. We are now ready to expound from that overview.

Like a built-in toolkit for parental self-regulation, conscious-parenting emphasizes tools that inherently help you to regulate. Not only will it help you cultivate a deeper relationship with your children, and yourself, it will also help you maintain an optimal level of self-regulation.

Here are the five conscious-parenting principles, plus how to use them:

1. Present-moment awareness. As much as possible, be fully present and engaged with your children, rather than being distracted by external concerns or preoccupations.

I understand that this is much easier said than done, but there's so much value in honoring and participating in the present moments in front of us. Parents have several responsibilities and demands, and too often, the mere consideration of those things robs us from the real present-moment awareness that actually gives us more joy and fulfillment, and helps to decrease stress and anxiety.

Here's what to do: Several times a day, remind yourself to "come back to the present moment." What does this mean? So often, we find our bodies in one place but our minds and attention in a completely different place. You may be in a meeting but thinking about dinner for tonight. You could be in bed but wondering about that weird interaction you had with someone last week.

You could be joining your child in an activity but truly thinking about all of the work you have to do when you all are done.

The goal here is to stay in the present as much as possible. So go ahead and set a few alarms or timers in your phone and title them "Come back to the present moment."

Want to take it up a notch? You can also develop a simple mindfulness practice. To start, choose five minutes out of your day when you simply focus on breathing, and see where that takes you.

2. Self-reflection. Engage in self-reflection and self-awareness to understand your triggers, emotions, and reactions. Doing so helps you to respond to your children in a calm and thoughtful manner.

Again, much easier said than done, but without this self-reflection, we are unable to truly process and understand the interactions we have with our children or others. Furthermore, without self-reflection, we also will never understand or even recognize the role we, ourselves, play in various experiences with our children. We won't be able to develop that deeper understanding of why we might be dysregulated or how that impacts our families.

While it may feel emotionally distressing to stop and think about things that may feel challenging or your most dysregulated moments, it allows for a much more expanded view of what is really going on and how to make some changes.

So here's what you can do: Pick a day or moment out of the week when you can commit to self-reflection. This can be as short or long as you'd like for it to be, but decide on a time frame that feels manageable and realistic for you. Additionally, you'll need to decide how you want to self-reflect, and the options are endless. You could journal, audio record your thoughts, think during a yoga or other movement session, or simply just sit in silence with your thoughts.

The goal here is to become comfortable with the process of self-reflection and learning how to consistently integrate it into your life.

3. Modeling behavior. Model the behavior you want to see in your children, including emotional intelligence, respect, and empathy.

The concept of modeling for parents is so transformative because it takes away some of the pressure many of us feel to teach certain skills to our children, especially when we, ourselves, have not mastered or fully understood those same skills. For example, many parents find themselves stressed out and on edge because they are struggling to help their children adopt a certain behavior or skill (e.g., self-regulation). These parents go through the process of looking online for help, reading through countless parenting articles for child behaviors. They may even go as far as to read a few books about the topic. Some even find podcasts to consume, with the hope of trying various strategies with their children at home.

These parents have the very best of intentions and admirable desires for supporting their children through some really tough behaviors, but they are unable to follow through because they, themselves, are already dysregulated and forgetting one of the most powerful learning tools all parents have access to—modeling.

The goal here is to focus less on teaching behaviors and instead placing much more of your focus on modeling those same behaviors. That means the focus will go from your child to yourself, which can feel scary and uncomfortable for some parents. I want you to trust the process in knowing that as you learn to truly adopt and internalize the behaviors or coping strategies you're hoping to see in your child, you'll be able to model them even better.

4. Embracing imperfection. Parenting can be a challenging journey with ups and downs. Therefore, approach parenting challenges with self-compassion and a willingness to learn and grow.

The idea of embracing imperfect parenting has been a challenging task for parents of this generation. Our experiences of parenting are so unique because we have much greater access to information, which allows for us to simply know more about child development, mental health, and the makings of healthy growth for children. Information is great, but sometimes access to too much information can bring a whole new challenge, such as the pressure to get it all right.

It has brought us comfort to rest on the belief that past generations maybe didn't get certain things right because they simply didn't know better. So what does it mean to be a generation of parents who do know better and still struggle to do all the right things?

The goal here is to begin shifting your belief about what it means to "do your best" as a parent. Instead, focus on "knowing better" meaning "doing better," and accept that even if you have more information, you will still make mistakes and maybe, that isn't something that needs to be fixed.

5. Cultivating gratitude. Practice gratitude and appreciation for the joys and challenges of parenting.

Simply put, find moments of joy, which often begin with gratitude. You all are fully aware of the ups and downs of parenthood, with the downs too often feeling like they might outweigh the ups. In seasons like this, gratitude may have to become more intentional, and a gratitude practice can come in handy.

The goal here is to cultivate moments where you are intentional and consistent about finding what you are grateful for as a parent. A practice I have enjoyed is this:

At the end of my day, I write down three things I am grateful for in that moment or from within that day. I've done this for several years, even before becoming a parent, and it always has a way of bringing much needed perspective when I need it the most.

This practice can always be modified. If you don't want to write, you can simply say the three things aloud or silently to yourself. If you are more of a morning person, you can do this first thing in the morning, or even during the day. Regardless of what time of day you do it, pick a time that will help you find some consistency. Also, if three doesn't feel like the right number for you, feel free to do more or less, but no more than five.

ACTIVE ENGAGEMENT IN RE-PARENTING

I met with a therapy client recently, and she let me know that she and her mother were not on great terms that week.

"She always overshares about her dating life and I hate that. It's a huge trigger for me," she explained to me as she began to tell about what actually happened with her mother.

"She was telling me about this man she likes and how he was making excuses about his schedule, why he couldn't see her, etc., and I just didn't care! So I said to her, 'Who cares?'"

I immediately looked at my client with shock in my eye and we both chuckled out loud. Her response took us both by surprise.

"Okay, I know we are laughing but really, tell me what about that is bothering you so much?" I asked her.

"It's because she always makes everything about herself," my client responded quickly.

"Growing up, she always made everything about herself. She would always tell me about men she's dating and completely overshare with adult information. It was always about her and never about me. There were so many times when I just needed her to see that I needed something but she never could. It was always about her. It's not fair."

My client and I finished that session exploring all the ways that her relationship with her mother felt unfair because, as a child, she never felt as if her mother was able to focus enough to notice when she was in need. We identified how that theme of "it's not fair" has continued to permeate into her adult life, where she now finds herself having moments that feel unjust and unfair when it comes to her own needs not being met. We were able to bridge the gap between these adult moments and the unmet emotional needs from her own childhood that need to be addressed and repaired.

"So this is what they mean when they say re-parenting? Wow, I have a lot to reflect on this week."

Just as it was with my client, this topic of re-parenting may also feel familiar to you. In chapter 5, I explained what re-parenting is, why it's important, and what four principles can help you along your re-parenting journey. Now, I want to revisit the topic because it is a very significant part of our journey to better self-regulation, just like it was for my client.

If you have struggled with chronic dysregulation for some time, it's quite possible that you may have some unmet needs that began in childhood. I understand how "woo woo" that all sounds, but trust me, it's a lot more common that people realize.

We were just talking about embracing imperfect parenthood, because none of us have had a perfect childhood. Just like we will continue to make mistakes, our parents have also made a ton of mistakes. Yes, some parents more than others. Yes, some of those mistakes are more traumatic than others. Regardless of how many mistakes or their severity, sometimes those mistakes can create wounds that go unhealed.

As a psychologist, it would be irresponsible of me to note that because you are able to identify an unhealed wound or need from childhood, that you have been "traumatized" or would meet clinical criteria for post-traumatic stress disorder. Experiencing an enduring hurt from childhood and also being traumatized in a way that leads one to develop a true clinical mental health condition are two separate things that can sometimes overlap. There may be some of you who have endured childhood harms so aggressive that you have developed PTSD and are still healing. However, most of you likely experienced hurts and pains in your past that maybe did not rise to the level of PTSD, and yet you still might greatly benefit from re-parenting. PTSD is not required.

Adulting is hard because so much is now your own responsibility, including your own healing. Re-parenting acknowledges that wounds may have occurred in your childhood and accepts that while your parents may have been partly responsible for those wounds, it's now up to you to make sure your wounds are healed.

My client went on a re-parenting journey, and maybe it's time for you to begin one too. What do you think?

Here's what I want you to do:

Take a few moments to consider whether there are any lingering, unmet emotional needs from your own childhood that need to be addressed and healed. If so, I invite you to go on a re-parenting journey and to take it seriously. You are the only one who can begin the process of healing these wounds, and I fully believe in your ability to do so.

Chapter 5 has everything you need to begin your journey. Refer back to it when you're ready, and prepare to meet the healed version of you on the other side.

THE CONSCIOUS TAKEAWAY

So what does this all mean? What are you doing all of this for?

You probably have noticed by now how much intention and reflection the Conscious Approach requires, and you're right—this feels like work. But I want to remind you of an important takeaway to keep you grounded as you go about this process in this approach.

The conscious takeaway is this: Why?

Yes, just a simple "why."

The big questions I want you to be ask yourself more than ever before are:

- What is the *why* behind my experience of parenting?
- What is the *why* behind my experience of my children?
- What is the *why* behind that big reaction I just had?
- What is the *why* behind this moment that I am in right now?

If you've ever had a two-year-old, then you know how important that question of *why* becomes. Young toddlers question everything, usually in the form of constantly asking that very question.

Often, there is a bigger and deeper why behind everything we experience, especially in parenting. So get curious (just like our two-year-olds) and ask why.

THE ULTIMATE GOAL

One last thing: Why did you decide to read this book? I'm sure I've asked you this before but I want to circle back and ask you one more time.

I have a suspicion that many of you have a very similar reason, and I decided to call this reason the Ultimate Goal.

I believe that goal is to preserve the connection and safety your child feels with you. However, somewhere along the way, things got hard and you started to wonder if the overwhelm, stress, overstimulation, anxiety, anger, and overall dysregulation was getting in the way of your child continuing to feel that connection and safety.

I know that's what you want, so from here on out, let's just make that the ultimate goal: You are on a forever journey in preserving the connection and safety your child feels with you and you both will be forever changed from this goal that you are grounding yourself in today.

Keep this question in mind as you continue to navigate tough parenting moments and mistakes: Do my actions and reactions align with my ultimate goal?

If yes, amazing.

If not, you now have the tools, and you can start again.

CHAPTER 13

• • •

The Realist Approach

When all else fails, let's just get real.

I've come a long way from that day in the bathroom, with the plunger.

Side note: Part of me is now wondering if I will be forever known as the mom psychologist who wrote a book about that time she yelled at her kid because of the plunger in the bathroom.

In any case, I've come a long way. I've learned the errors of my ways. I've developed some new skills. I've deepened my relationship with myself and connected with my own childhood wounds. I've developed a practical plan for managing and coping with my triggers for dysregulation. I also have a plan for how to commit to constant re-parenting. I am taking accountability for my mistakes while also giving myself an abundance of grace. I can handle a lot more tough moments without panicking or freaking out like I used to. I feel really proud of the parent I've evolved into. I love who I've become. I love who I am becoming. I finally feel like maybe I really am exactly who my children need.

...and I still yell sometimes.

I still get upset and then realize my reaction was bigger than it should have been.

I still have moments when I could have listened better or responded in a gentler way.

I still get overwhelmed when both of my children are talking to me or even talking loudly to each other.

I still get overstimulated in the evenings after work, and sometimes it means I zone out and spend too much time on my phone.

To put it briefly, I'm still making mistakes. Far fewer mistakes, absolutely. Zero mistakes, absolutely not.

I'm still making mistakes, and even after you're completely finished with this book, you will too. Today, we are promising one another that we will no longer fight against the mistakes that are simply bound to happen.

THE REALIST APPROACH

The third and final approach within the PCR Method is the Realist Approach. It is the one where we acknowledge that we've done all we can, we've tried our best, and we are letting the rest go.

Yes, I'm serious. Let that shit go.

A significant part of the Realist Approach is learning how to accept some of the hard truths that come with the reality of parenting. You can begin to do that by understanding a concept that is far too underrated in the mental health world—radical acceptance.

RADICAL ACCEPTANCE

I'll be honest, when I first learned about the concept of radical acceptance in graduate school, I didn't give it much attention. It felt like the most common-sensical solution but also one that should be saved as a last resort. I often believed that if we were resorting to radical acceptance, then we were giving up in some way, and I wasn't about to be the therapist who simply helped my clients to give up on fixing things.

I was wrong, and thankfully, I've evolved since then, because now, as a more seasoned psychologist who is also a parent, I've come to understand that maybe radical acceptance needs to be the first step. How do you know what to work on or change if you haven't first accepted what is?

Historically speaking, radical acceptance is a concept often associated with a form of therapy called dialectical behavior therapy (DBT), which is a type of cognitive behavioral herapy developed by Dr. Marsha Linehan. Radical acceptance is a therapeutic technique that encourages individuals to fully and completely accept reality, especially when they are facing difficult or distressing situations.

Funnily enough, radical acceptance has been found to be particularly helpful for people who struggle with emotional regulation, or intense emotional reactions to challenging life circumstances.

Does that sound familiar?

At its core, the idea of radical acceptance is to acknowledge and embrace reality, even when it's painful or undesirable. The goal is to accept this reality without judgment or resistance. In other words, radical acceptance means accepting the present moment as it is, rather than fighting or denying it. It's also important to mention accepting the present moment does not mean that you have to like or condone the challenging situation happening around you. Rather, you are recognizing it as a fact that cannot be changed in the present moment.

ACCEPT THE THINGS YOU CANNOT CHANGE

When I was growing up, my father loved the Serenity Prayer. As someone who grew up Christian but now doesn't particularly identify in any religious manner, I can still appreciate the ideas behind that prayer. I began to understand it even more so as a parent who struggled to manage and regulate myself for so long.

The first part of that prayer asks for serenity to accept the things that we cannot change. To me, that means finding peace among the things that I may also hold some discontentment with. It also means experiencing calm as I navigate and experience these things that I cannot be completely happy with. Last, this part of the prayer means giving up the fight against these things and allowing them to be.

I took some time to think of all the things that I believe parents often struggle to accept. Here's what I came up with:

1. There is not enough time, and much of it will be for someone else.

2. I will not always enjoy parenting.

3. I will make mistakes.

4. I will not always be happy.

5. My kids will not always be happy.

6. My house will be a mess most of the time.

7. My kids may not always like me.

8. My marriage/partnership/relationships may become strained at some point.

9. Things will not be as routine and consistent as they used to be.

10. I will become overwhelmed.

11. I will become overstimulated.

12. I may experience rage and resentment as a parent.

13. I will not always be able to protect my kids from everything.

14. I have changed and will continue to change.

15. I miss who I used to be and may continue to miss who I used to be.

16. I may miss and grieve my life before having kids.

17. Being a parent may feel triggering.

18. I will not always have the answers, and that will feel scary.

19. People (including my own parents) won't always be able to support us.

20. I may never feel like I have enough support.

What's on your list? More importantly, how long have you been fighting against what's on your list?

Next, how would it feel to no longer fight what's on your list?

What would it mean to move into a space of deeper acceptance for the things that have changed and that cannot be controlled in this present moment?

FEARS THAT BLOCK RADICAL ACCEPTANCE

What if I told you that part of the reason why you haven't accepted some of the things that come with being a parent is fear?

On the surface, it may seem that there is another reason why so many of us hold on so tightly to things that we should let go of. However, in my years of supporting others regarding their mental and emotional health, fear is sneaky yet pervasive. Fear has a way of masking and pretending to be some other rational, logical reason for why something should be done or a decision should be made in a certain way. Fears often keep us holding onto things so tightly that we don't realize that letting go would bring the relief we've been needing. Here are a few that I believe are common among parents, and affirmations to help soothe the fear.

I'm afraid that I'm not trying my best or haven't given it my all.

What if your attempts at radical acceptance are being blocked because you are afraid of failure? What if you believe that if you can't or haven't accomplished some version of parenthood by now, that you will fail, and that leads you to continue to persist at trying to change what is ultimately unable to be changed?

Affirmations for fears of failure:
• "Mistakes are opportunities for growth and learning."

- "I am resilient, and I can handle setbacks."
- "Failure does not define me; my actions and persistence do."
- "I release the need for perfection and embrace my imperfections."
- "I have the courage to face my fears and move forward."

I'm afraid that I may harm my child.

What if you haven't yet embraced radical acceptance because you believe that accepting some version of yourself will ultimately harm your child? What if you believe that if you can't change yourself or something about yourself, then you will not be able to be a good parent to your child?

Affirmations for doubtful parenting:
- "I trust in my parenting abilities and believe in myself."
- "I release self-doubt and embrace self-belief."
- "I am enough just as I am."
- "I trust my intuition and make decisions with confidence."
- "I am constantly growing and learning, and I believe in my potential."

I'm afraid of how this will affect my future or my family's future.

What if you are still resisting radical acceptance because you are unsure of how the current circumstance or situation will affect the future? What if uncertainty is too hard for you to bear and instead you are still attempting to control it, when we ultimately may not have the answers?

Affirmations for soothing fears of uncertainty:

- "I embrace the unknown and trust that it holds opportunities for growth."
- "I release the need for control and surrender to the flow of life."
- "I am resilient and adaptable, even in uncertain times."
- "I find peace in the present moment, regardless of what the future holds."
- "I trust that the universe has a plan for me, even if I can't see it yet."

I'm afraid that this is all there is to my life.

What if you haven't yet tried radical acceptance because you're afraid that life will disappoint you? What if you had high hopes and expectations for how life would look or feel and none of it has come to pass? What if you feel as if you will be giving in to a life that may bring more heartbreak by accepting the truth?

Affirmations for disappointment:

- "I acknowledge my disappointment and allow myself to feel it."
- "Disappointment is a natural part of life, and it doesn't define my worth."
- "I choose to focus on what I can learn from this experience."
- "I trust that better things are on the horizon."
- "I am open to new opportunities and possibilities."

"I'm afraid that this will never get any easier or better."

What if you haven't yet come around to the idea of radical accep-tance because you are so afraid that life will never get better? What if you have been longing for the moment for things to feel easier and you believed that if you kept working to change things, that feeling of ease would finally come? What if accept-ing now feels like accepting more difficulty?

Affirmations for tough times:

- "I trust in my ability to navigate through difficult situations."
- "I choose to focus on what I can control and let go of what I can't."
- "This too shall pass, and I will emerge with greater wisdom and strength."
- "I am resilient, and I am capable of finding solutions and moving forward."
- "I have the courage to face adversity and come out on the other side."

STEPS TOWARD MORE RADICAL ACCEPTANCE

I hope you are starting to see that radical acceptance will be a valuable and necessary tool for your journey of improving your self-regulation abilities and reducing dysregulation. As you begin to practice radical acceptance more, you'll be more likely to let go of fruitless efforts to change things that are beyond your control and will be better able to focus on constructive, healthy responses to the challenges you will continue to face.

Radical acceptance is about acknowledging and embracing reality as it is, without judgment or resistance. Here are the steps to get there:

- **Acknowledge reality:** Begin today with finding a deeper acknowledgment for the reality of your situation. This means recognizing and accepting what is happening, even if it's painful or uncomfortable.

- **Let go of resistance:** Stop fighting against the reality of today's situation. Your resistance will lead to increased suffering and distress. Instead, release your resistance and embrace what is.

- **Understand you can't change the past:** You cannot change the past. Accepting this fact can help you let go of regrets and resentments related to these past events that continue to haunt you.

- **Focus on the present:** Shift your focus to the present moment. Radical acceptance encourages mindfulness, which means being fully present in the here and now.

- **Embrace uncertainty:** Life is inherently uncertain, and you cannot control everything, regardless of how much you'd like to try. Embrace the uncertainty and impermanence of life.

- **Avoid "should" statements:** Try to avoid saying things like "I should have done this differently" or "It shouldn't be like this." These statements create resistance and judgment. Instead, accept that things are as they are.

- **Practice self-compassion:** Treat yourself with kindness and compassion. Recognize that you are doing the best you can with the resources and knowledge you have.

CHAPTER 14

• • •

BONUS Tools for Parental Self-Regulation

Wow, what a ride this has been.

I don't know about you, but I have truly enjoyed my time with you as we have navigated this journey together. I know when you first picked up this book, you probably wondered if this would be the thing to finally help you beat dysregulation for good. Now that we are near the end, my hope is that you can confidently say yes to this book being the answer you've needed to solve the issue of chronic dysregulation. I'm so excited for you to begin practicing all that you've learned to better self regulate and then begin to model this for your children too.

I know that we've covered so much, but there are still a few quick tools that I really enjoy and value for improved self-regulation capacity and ability. So I decided to end part III of our time together with some BONUS tools to further add to your newly formed toolkit.

I recommend using these tools in collaboration with any portion of the PCR Method. These tools can also be used as quick refreshers when you need something right away. However, be cautious not to get into a habit of using only tools. While they can be helpful momentarily, they truly need to be added to a complete system or plan for long-term management of your dysregulation cycles, which is exactly what the PCR Method is for.

Remember, you have everything you need and more. Now let's keep adding to your toolkit so that you can be on your way.

BACK TO THE BASICS

How often have you felt grumpy, upset, anxious, down, and low energy and wondered what was going on? You kept pressing forward, meeting deadlines, showing up for your family, continuing to do all the things and noticed that you continued to feel worse. You wondered more and more whether something is wrong and started to research and explore what it could be. Your Google search and brain have wandered to the ends of the Earth with possibilities of what could be wrong with you, making you feel more overwhelmed than ever.

There are times when dysregulation could be a result of bigger, more complex issues that need to be addressed; however, there are many other times when dysregulation is a function of lacking basic self-care. When this is the case, it's time to get back to the basics by checking in on the following:

1. SLEEP

Are you sleeping? If the answer is no, set your intentions on restabilizing your sleep, with the goal of seeking six to eight hours per night. Of course, there will be nights when you fall short of that goal, but the intention is to get as close to that range as consistently as you are able to.

Have a newborn or a child who is still waking in the middle of the night? If so, come back to this goal once your child's sleep routines have been solidified, because remember—we are not fighting against the realities of the current moment. Now is the time to accept that sleep will be fleeting and instead focus on the plethora of other self-regulation tools you now have.

2. HYDRATION

Are you adequately hydrated? If you've paused to answer, then it is likely no. If you are doubtful of whether you're adequately hydrating your body, set the intention to reestablish a hydration routine. Decide on the beverages (water is my personal favorite) that will help you satisfy this goal, as well as how you will make sure that reminders are available to help you meet this goal.

Reminders for hydration might include a few timers on your phone or watch, asking you to drink water. Another might be a constant sticky note on your desk, with that same ask for water. Or you can enlist the support of friends and loved ones to help hold you accountable. Regardless of the method you choose, drink up!

3. FOOD

Are you eating? Also, are you eating the right foods? As you consider these questions, I want to make it clear that I am not advocating for any type of diet or particular eating plan. Rather, my goal for you is to eat, eat regularly, and be intentional about whether the foods you are consuming align with your overall mental and physical health goals.

Parenting is challenging, and it's almost impossible to do a good job if you are not adequately fueled. Begin thinking of food as the fuel that gets and keeps you going. Without it, you will not be able to carry out the full list of responsibilities and heavy demands you carry on a daily basis. Now may be the time to truly take inventory of what eating looks like for you and if your relationship with food needs some tweaks.

4. MOVEMENT

Are you moving your body? If yes, how much and can you move more? If no, now is the time to reenergize your body with regular movement. I understand that the reality for most parents is one that involves some form of work. You may work in an office or from home, but regardless of what that work looks like, many of us are not moving our bodies enough as we navigate our days. Consider how you might be able to start moving your body more throughout your day.

Did you notice that I did not say "exercise"? That was on purpose, because many of us have various feelings about exercise and often that word comes with a sense of demand or burden that I know you don't need. Instead, think about movement, which should feel more freeing, flexible, and attainable. Consider how you might be able to get in a few more steps, take the actual steps, or stretch more on your breaks. Either way, get moving.

Back to the Basics DISCLAIMER: I know some of you may feel tempted to attack all of these basic self-care goals at once, because let's be real, it's possible that all of these needs are being neglected. That happens; however, focusing on all of these steps simultaneously is not something I recommend.

Instead, start from the top and work your way through, only proceeding to the next step once you've made your best effort at progress in the previous step.

BREATH

"Mommy! I need to show you something!"

"Yes? What do you need to show me?"

"This!"

My son immediately took a few steps back and placed his palms together at his chest. He closed his eyes and took a big depth breath, while bringing his palms up above his head and out into the shape of a rainbow.

"It's a rainbow breath! My teacher showed us today."

I was stunned. Had my son just taught me a breathing skill that I hadn't yet known about?

"Wow, baby, that was cool. Show me again."

By now, my daughter had joined in too, and we both watched as he took another big step back, placed his palms together at his chest, and completed his rainbow breath.

"I can do a rainbow breath too," said my daughter, as she proceeded to also show me her biggest and best rainbow breath.

Within seconds, we all were taking rainbow breaths together and discussing all the reasons why one would need to stop and take a rainbow breath. We talked about how feelings like frustration, anger, worry, fear, and even sadness may just need a few rainbow breaths to eventually get better. We have been doing rainbow breaths together ever since.

Aside from tending to your basic self-care needs, breath is another of the most basic regulation tools you carry with you every day. Its simplicity is partly why many of us tend to undermine how important breathing can be for self-regulation. If it's so simple, how could it possibly help? How could something so small ease some of the big worries and burdens you carry daily?

The magic in breath is not its ability to make all of your cares and worries go away. Rather, breath is powerful because of its ability to quickly bring you to the here and now. Focusing on the one thing your body naturally does for you second by second helps you to get to the most present moment possible, and you'll find that there are often very few worries and concerns in the true present. Often, your fears, worries, overwhelm, and dysregulation are a combination of several cognitive experiences that are focused in the past or in the future. Breath invites you to journey to the present for a much-needed retreat and reprieve.

If you want breath to feel more magical, consider making it a consistent practice. Take a moment to figure out where in your daily routine you can pause simply to focus on breathing, because we don't have to stop and breathe only when we are struggling. Making mindful breathing a consistent practice will allow you to have more of the special trips to the present, which ultimately helps you to better regulate your mind and body for the long haul.

GO OUTSIDE

When was the last time you went outside?

Not just to get into a car, or to grab a package. I'm not even talking about quick errands that force you to get outside.

When was the last time you intentionally decided you were going to go outside because you just knew it would be good for you?

If it's been a while, then this one might be for you.

One of the more positive ways that the COVID-19 pandemic changed my life was that it introduced me to the outdoors in a very new way. I know you remember exactly how challenging and traumatic the pandemic was. In some ways, it almost felt as if time slowed down and all of the spaces that once felt safe were now considered dangerous. Safety was truly left to your own home and the outdoors.

Outside became one of my new safe spaces. When I didn't feel safe going to my friends' or loved ones' homes, I knew that we could go outside and be that much safer. When I missed going to the movies or missed a time when I could go to the grocery store and not feel afraid, I knew I still had the nearby parks to explore. When I was tired and feeling stuck in the house with my husband and infant, I knew I could escape on a stroll around the neighborhood and come back feeling refreshed.

At the time, I thought the outdoors was just my new safe space, but eventually I started to learn and understand a lot more about the actual healing powers of nature. Endless studies have proven the positive effects that nature can have on our mental, physical, and emotional health. Some of these effects include:

- Increased feelings of pleasure
- Sharper focus and concentration
- Enhanced physical relaxation
- Decreased stress, anxiety, tension, and anger
- Boosts in creativity and problem-solving skills
- Reduced cortisol levels
- Lowered heart rate and blood pressure
- Increased vitamin D levels
- Lowered risk for depression
- Improved sleep quality

For many of us, even just a few of these benefits could be life-altering, and it seems that getting outside more is a gateway to achieve them. So when are you going to go outside?

I want you to take some time to consider how you might be able to increase the amount of time you spend outdoors, and remember, you can keep this simple. How could you spend an extra five to ten minutes outside today, tomorrow, or the next day? That's all it takes.

SENSORY OFFLOADING

Okay, so I made this up.

...and yes, I know that this is a book I've written so I've made all of this up, but this one, I really made up. Let me explain.

I want you to take a second to imagine the last time you were feeling extremely overstimulated and probably also very dysregulated. In that moment, what was going on? What was happening around you?

A time that comes up for me is an evening after work, when I was standing in the middle of my kitchen while my children were whizzing past me on their mini cars. I hadn't been able to change out of my work clothes just yet and felt stuffed in my non-stretchy pants. The dog was barking, my husband's podcast was way too loud on his phone's speaker, and there was stuff everywhere. The TV was on and watching itself, the sound of the air humidifier was on ten, the lights were too bright, and my brain had simply had enough.

My senses were overloaded, and believe it or not, this often becomes a common, everyday occurrence for many parents. We have become accustomed to this level of sensory overload and in the long term, it can have some pretty negative effects on our ability and capacity for self-regulation.

Sensory offloading is a way to help soothe your senses when they are feeling completely overwhelmed, and it's simply releasing or reducing the amount of experience our senses are having.

What senses am I referring to? While most of us have five senses, when it comes to dysregulation, I believe the following to be the biggest culprits:

- **Sound:** i.e., there is too much noise.
- **Sight:** i.e., my environment looks chaotic.
- **Touch:** i.e., my physical body feels uncomfortable.

So how can you start to turn down the volume (literally and figuratively) on your senses? Here are a few of my favorite ways:

SENSES	OFFLOADING STRATEGY
Sound	• Wear noise-canceling headphones or earbuds. • Turn off or turn down the volume on devices and appliances. • Enforce "quiet time" at home with your family. • Go outside (to where the noise is often more pleasant and less invasive). • Turn on white noise or other ambient sounds.
Sight	• Turn off or turn down the intensity of artificial lights. • Clear up unnecessary clutter. • Take a few minutes to simply close your eyes or wear an eye mask. • Put on sunglasses. • Escape to a space that visually looks more pleasing or comforting.
Touch	• Change into clothes that feel more comfortable. • Wear comfortable slippers or soft socks. • Enforce "rest" or "stillness" at home with your family. • Let your loved ones know when you need physical space. • Give yourself or ask someone else to give you a big hug.

COREGULATION

Sometimes you just need a hug.

My children taught me that very real truth, and while I knew that people often benefit from physical touch and closeness from others, I couldn't really appreciate it until I saw how quickly my child was able to calm down from a temper tantrum or big feelings simply by receiving a hug from me.

Many times, they don't even need a hug, and all it takes for them to regain composure after having a hard time is for me to sit next to them, rub their back, or acknowledge and validate that I see that they are upset and it is, in fact, okay to feel that way.

Simply being present with them as they are having a hard time helps them navigate the wave of big feelings, and then they are ready to tackle the rest of their day, better and stronger than before.

These experiences with them helped me to more seriously consider the power and potential in coregulation and what it could mean or look like for parents. If our children benefit from coregulation so much, why wouldn't we?

Coregulation can be thought of as the process through which people access the ability to soothe and manage distressing emotions and sensations through connection with others.

Watching my children coregulate with me helped me realize that parents may also be able to better access the ability and capacity for regulation in the safety and comfort of another. It feels good to know that we are not alone and that there is someone who can bear witness to the challenges we may be facing, offer support, and show that they care. Even just someone's presence sitting with you or simply being on the phone can feel comforting in a moment of distress.

So how will you begin to regulate in the presence of another? Here are a few simple options for you to consider:

- Actively listen to a loved one share something positive about their day.
- Open up to a loved one about the challenges of your day.
- Ask a loved one to help you solve a problem.
- Invite a loved one to go on a walk with you.
- Engage in deep breathing or another form of mindfulness with a loved one.
- Participate in a shared activity with a loved one.
- Seek out a hug or another form of physical affection from a loved one.

I'm excited for you to practice and experience how pleasant coregulation can feel with someone you trust.

CHAPTER 15

• • •

One Last Thing

Hey, how'd you get this book?

Can you even read?

Well, since you're here, I want to share a secret with you. I don't know if you know but there is someone who really cares about you.

They bought this book and read the entire thing from front to back. The whole time they were reading, they were thinking of you.

Yep, I promise! They were even thinking about you when they bought the book. They picked this book up because they wanted you to know just how much they love you and hoped that this book would help.

They read the entire thing and they have learned so many new things! They learned more about themselves, how to help themselves feel better when they are having a hard day, and also how to make sure that other days don't feel so hard. They even learned a few new things about you too, and I'm sure that soon, they are going to try and teach you some of the new things they learned.

I'm really proud of them for doing this. I know how important it was for them to work on feeling better but also being better—

for you. You may not know it now, but one day– you're going to feel really proud of them too. Your parent is working so hard to provide the best life for you, and I know that one day, you'll see it and love them all the more for it.

You may not know or realize it now, but they spend a lot of time thinking of you and honestly, everything they do is for you. They love you more than you can even imagine, even when they are having a bad day. They also really love you when you're having a bad day. Honestly, they will love you forever. There is nothing you could do to make them stop.

You have the very best parent in the entire world, and I'm so happy and excited for you to be able to spend every day with them.

Could you do me a favor?

Well, I've spent quite a bit of time with them as they've read this book. We've had a lot of conversations, and I see how hard they can be on themselves. Sometimes, they just don't see how good of a job they're doing. They have a big job, and I know that taking care of you and everything else isn't always easy, despite how easy they make it seem. I guess what I'm trying to say is, could you do me a favor and let them know every now and then that they are doing amazing?

Let them know that even when they are having a hard day or when they've made a mistake, it's still such a pleasure and joy to be with them each day.

And if you ever notice that they may not feel as happy, give them a big hug to remind them that they mean everything to you, because I know they do.

Okay, it was really nice to meet you, and you have the best parent in this world!

Until next time.

Acknowledgments

Thank you to Ashley Brown for opening the doors of possibility for this project. I'm deeply thankful to my Ulysses Press team for their support and encouragement. Special thanks to Brandi for her meticulous attention to detail in interpreting our research data. Thank you to all participants of the Self-Regulation in Parenting Research Study; your invaluable feedback shaped this book. To my husband, family, and friends, your unwavering love sustained me.

Last, to my son, Cedric. May this book forever symbolize our shared journey of growth.

About the Author

Dr. Amber Thornton is a licensed clinical psychologist and strong advocate for the mental health and well-being of parents. Dr. Amber loves writing and creating content online that will speak to the everyday struggles of motherhood and parenthood.

Dr. Amber holds a BS in psychology from the Ohio State University and a PsyD in clinical psychology from Wright State University School of Professional Psychology. She's an Ohio native who has made Washington, DC, her home since 2018. She loves spending time with her husband and two children.

Connect with Dr. Amber Thornton on Instagram or YouTube @dramberthornton. Learn more about her work by visiting her website at www.dramberthornton.com.